THE CONTINUOUS FLAME

THE CONTINUOUS FLAME
Teilhard in the Great Traditions

Edited by

Harry J. Cargas

St. Louis University

B. HERDER BOOK CO.

314 N. Jefferson, St. Louis, Missouri

Library of Congress Catalog Card No. 73-109-440

For Jessie Teilhard Cargas

In Whom The Flame Continually Burns

CONTENTS

INTRODUCTION

Critics of Teilhard de Chardin frequently place him in one of two categories. Some accuse him of not being an original thinker, of merely being an eclectic, an assimilator if you will — as if there were some evil in that. Would that more of humanity would be much more eclectic than it is, the problems resulting either through one-sidedness or some other form of ignorance being enormous.

Other critics, perhaps those who feel most "threatened" by the French Jesuit's writings, lay on the charge of heresy in the sense that heresy is the ultimate sin. It would be superfluous to point out how many writers who are now considered to be orthodox in relation to Catholic teaching were branded somewhere in history as Satan's messengers.

The purpose of this book, hopefully, speaks to both of the above points. Both charges can hardly be correct. An eclectic is one who synthesizes the thinking of others. But almost by definition it means, if the writer under discussion is in any way worthwhile, the eclectic has chosen the best, the most useful, the truest, the most provable. This is, of course, not the description of the heretic. The eclectic is somehow in a tradition; those in heresy are not.

What the essays in this book show, it is hoped, is that indeed Teilhard is an eclectic, but one of the most adventurous and exciting synthesizers in modern history. He is in a double Christian tradition, the tradition of being orthodox and in tune with the great religious and secular movements in history as well as in the great tradition of advancing already established tradition further forward. Christian thinking, like any other thinking, cannot remain unmoved for very long. The danger of stagnation, of irrelevancy, is too imminent. What was needed in this era, and what Teilhard has provided, is what may be described as an original eclecticism.

This is a curious time when young rebel protesters of various kinds are being scoffed at for not keeping some touch with the past. They lack a sense of continuity, of history, of how their current situation has come about. Teilhard, often categorized as a rebel, is surely the most aware man of where he has come from. It is this, indeed, that has characterized his knowing where he, and we, are going. The traditions he represents to us are the basis for his thinking, for his projections, yes for even his guesses.

A look at the contents of this book will show how the essays collected here attempt to support the thesis of this Introduction. Teilhard is seen, in some aspects at least, in relation to such writers so apparently diverse as St. Paul and Marshall McLuhan, so apparently diverse as Tennyson and Jung.

We need not have limited ourselves to the authors contained herein. We might, for example, have extracted something on Teilhard and the great personalist philosopher Emmanuel Mounier from Andre Ligneul's book *Teilhard and Personalism*. As the author mentions in his first chapter, "Teilhard on several occasions characterized the direction needed to save humanity as 'personalism.' He was tired of seeing so many men fall back 'into a traditional conservatism,' and this places him in perfect accord with Mounier."

Others have noticed illuminating similarities between Teilhard and St. Bonaventure, Teilhard and Pascal, Teilhard and St. Thomas. Karl Stern has written that "It is quite possible that later generations may look on Teilhard as a St. Augustine of natural history." More contemporarily, the relationships of Teilhard and Bergson, Karl Rahner and President

Leopold Sedar Senghor of Senegal have at least been hinted at. This last mentioned statesman and poet said in a message:

Much more manifestly than in the last century, there has appeared the irresistible march of Humanity towards at the same time its 'totalization' and 'socialization,' to use the terms of Pierre Teilhard de Chardin. This is evidenced by science particularly in the development of the means of production. It isn't only men and material goods that cross frontiers but even more, ideas, techniques and mores; I mean civilization.

(Nor is this an isolated reference by Senghor to Teilhard. His thought is deeply influenced by Teilhard and he gladly admits to this.)

Essays that have been and could be written about Teilhard and others would include writers from many disciplines: theology, philosophy, letters, and psychology and several of the natural sciences. There could be profitable pieces on the Jesuit and Gabriel Marcel, Harvey Cox, Charles Darwin, Graham Greene, Oscar Cullman to begin a roster. Such poets as Richard Crashaw (in a discussion of *The Divine Milieu*) and Daniel Berrigan, a Jesuit who has read all of Teilhard, also belong on such a list.

Hopefully, then, the idea has been expressed. Teilhard is not a freak who happened at one instant in the twentieth century. He is both a culminating point (in that he is the conscious product of what went before) and a commencing point from which we can launch out into the future with hope, with joy, and with love.

HARRY J. CARGAS

ST. PAUL AND
TEILHARD DE CHARDIN
James H. Adams, OSFS

"All reality, even material reality, around each one of us, exists for our souls . . . (and) through our souls, for God in our Lord."[1]

This is the conclusion to which Pierre Teilhard de Chardin was drawn by his observation, even from his childhood days, that God's "invisible attributes are clearly seen — especially his everlasting power and divinity . . . through the things that are made."[2]

The materialism prevalent in modern philosophy denies the very existence of any form of reality apart from the material world. On the other hand, Christian reactions both to pantheism and to Manichaeism have tended to affirm the sovereign existence of a spiritual world distinct from the material world, and Christian asceticism, itself tinged to some extent with Manichaeism, has cemented the dichotomy. Meanwhile St. Paul seems to contradict materialism, Manichaeism, and the Christian attitude toward pantheism when he gives us a picture of all creation moving toward a state of total subjection to Christ at the end of time. For he plainly states that on the last day, God will be "all in all" — *en pasin panta Theos.*[3]

While it is clear that Paul is not a pantheist, at least in the sense that he would identify God and matter, there does

From *Salesian Studies,* 3 (Autumn, 1966): 8-14. Reprinted by permission of the publisher.

remain the problem of justifying the relationship he posits between the two. Teilhard has been accused of teaching pantheism, among other things, even though it is equally clear that he never had the intention of making that fatal identification. Whether the source of the accusation is a flaw in his philosophical system or in the interpretation of it is not the object of this study. Our purpose is rather to show how St. Paul formed the basis of Teilhard's teaching on matter, and nothing more.

Paul and Teilhard have much in common. Both were in love with Christ, both longed to share their love with others, especially with non-believers. Paul strove to put the language of the Scriptures into words that could be understood by the Epicureans and the Stoics to whom he was speaking. "He relieves 'the whole,' 'the one,' 'the origin,' 'life,' 'breath,' from the implication they have in Stoic thought with impersonal cosmic forces" and "instead he brings these realities into the same circuit, so to speak, as the personal creative force of God."[4] Similarly, Teilhard, confronted with his own observations from nature and the message of Christ as expressed by St. Paul, "sought to preach Christ to the de-Christianized Gentiles of his own day."[5] His interpretation of the theory of an evolution not ending with man but transcending him demanded a re-evaluation of our concept of matter. Its proper understanding is nothing less than the new frontier with which contemporary Christianity is confronted, a highway leading to the inauguration of an entirely renewed Christian era, which we can clearly see on the horizon.

Jewish tradition, based on divine revelation, had imposed on the Chosen People strict rules regarding uncleanliness or impurity resulting from the use of certain foods, from moral transgressions, contact with pagans, and even from some normal human processes such as childbirth. These injunctions had led to a bias against matter in general. In his attempt to explain that Christian morality involves a Christian orientation of all the intrinsically good pagan values,[6] Paul knew that he had to dethrone this fallacious generalization. In his

2

letter to the Romans[7] and again in the letter to Titus[8] Paul proclaimed the truth that "nothing is in itself unclean." It is quite clear that Paul is speaking not only of foods, but of all "taboos." "There is no objective reality in taboos of any kind. . . . Nothing is in itself unclean; only, anything is unclean for a man who considers it unclean."[9]

This last sentence is important. It places the Jewish condemnation of matter on a purely subjective level: material things are good or evil insofar as they are used for good or evil ends. In fact, material goods are even made holy when a thanksgiving is pronounced over them,[10] as Jesus did at the Last Supper. This teaching is not Paul's own; he holds it " 'in the Lord Jesus' — that is to say it is something inseparable from his Christian experience."[11]

Nevertheless a certain contempt for matter continued to pervade Christian asceticism through the centuries. As we have said, it was Teilhard's task to demonstrate in contemporary, scientific terms how the materialism that threatens the present world is in fact destined to be conquered by Christ. And he called upon the authority of St. Paul to support his argument: "By virtue of the Creation and, still more, of the Incarnation, nothing here below is profane for those who know how to see. On the contrary, everything is sacred to those capable of distinguishing that portion of chosen being which is subject to the attraction of Christ in the process of consummation."[12]

We can hardly justify Teilhard's sanctification of matter simply by giving a scriptural basis for the transcendental goodness of matter. Merely possessing that quality is too passive; if matter is to have ascetic value it has to be active, part of a dynamism toward the fulfillment of a goal.

For Paul there is only one goal, namely the Parousia, the second coming of Christ. On the level of the individual, he liked to think of it in terms of a prize to be won after successfully finishing an athletic contest, as in Philippians 3:13-14: ". . . forgetting what is past, I strain toward what is ahead. With my eyes fixed on the goal, I press on to the prize in store for those who have received from above God's call in Jesus Christ." Then, applying this same context to mankind as a whole, he encourages the Philippians by reminding them of the glorious day when Jesus will subject the entire universe to himself and will refashion "our lowly bodies, conforming them to his glorious body."[13] As Cerfaux puts it, having "summed up" in himself all that had been created by him and for him, now he exists with his Father as the sum of all things.[14]

Keeping this in mind, let us turn our attention to a curious expression we encountered in Teilhard's remark above: nothing is profane to him who knows how to see. Teilhard once described the object of his work as "an attempt to see . . . what happens to man, and what conclusions are forced upon us, when he is placed . . . in the framework of phenomenon."[15] By way of definition, Teilhard explained that the goal of man's whole "mysterious gift of existence" depends on "fuller being," and fuller being "can only increase through an increase of consciousness, that is to day in vision."[16]

What sense can we make out of this apparent vicious circle of terms? We have "vision," "existence," "fuller being," and "consciousness." At the very end of his fundamental work, *The Phenomenon of Man,* he tells us just what the conclusion is that has been "forced upon us":

By partially immersing himself in things . . . Christ . . . put himself in the position to subdue under himself, to purify, to direct and super-animate the general ascent of consciousness. And when he has gathered everything together and transformed everything, he will close in upon himself and his conquests, thereby rejoining, in a final gesture, the divine focus he has never left. Then, as St. Paul tells us, God shall be all in all.[17]

Does this not make it evident, then, that St. Paul and Teilhard both have the same objective in mind, namely to show how the entire material world can and must be used to proclaim the glory of God, that this end was in fact the very reason for its creation? Not only is the worth of the material world affirmed, but matter itself is ennobled by its participation in so holy a project, its sanctification in view of becoming part of God's new creation.[18]

Both Teilhard and St. Paul see this process of sanctification in progress at the present moment. Paul describes how "up to the present . . . the whole of creation has been groaning together as it undergoes the pains of childbirth. And not only creation, but we ourselves also groan in our hearts . . . waiting for the full adoption that will come to us through the redemption of our bodies."[19]

In like manner, Teilhard has viewed God's creation as sacred and capable of instructing us concerning the plan of the creator. "In this he stands in the most authentic, venerable, and constant biblical and Christian tradition, as it was formulated by St. Paul himself."[20] Teilhard's work is dedicated to the study of the cosmic, physical, biological, anthropological conditions that define this maturing of creation, through which it becomes capable of receiving the fullness of its supernatural end.

The subjective aspect of matter mentioned above is implied by Teilhard when he expresses the need of knowing how to "see." The implication is that one may not know how to "see," that is to "see" how material goods can be used so that they make a positive contribution to the conditions necessary for the fulfillment of the Parousia. "The time has come," he says, "to realize that an interpretation of the universe — even a positive one — remains unsatisfying unless it covers the interior as well as the exterior of things; mind as well as matter."[21]

By matter Teilhard means not exactly "the abstract entities defined under the name of science and philosophy," but also "the assemblage of things, energies, and creatures"[22] that fill the earth, reality in its widest possible sense. To determine just how St. Paul would concur with Teilhard, we may turn again to his letter to the Romans: "Now we know that for those who love God all things work together unto good."[23] We should be aware of the broad sense in which

Paul intended "all things" to be understood. For as Chrysostom interprets, "all things" refers especially to "tribulation, or poverty, or imprisonment, or famines, or deaths, or anything else whatsoever come upon us."[24] While Teilhard is aware that the world can just as well be the ruin of man: "Matter, you in whom I find both seduction and strength, you in whom I find blandishment and virility, you who can enrich and destroy . . ."[25] Chrysostom affirms: "if men who have learned to be philosophic can use the things of nature to the opposite of their intention, . . . much more will God work for those that love Him both these and also greater things by far. . . . As then things seemingly harmful do good to these, so do even things profitable harm those who love Him not."[26]

According to Teilhard, then, true Christian asceticism in the spirit of St. Paul no longer consists in liberating and purifying oneself from matter (a sentiment more Manichaean than Christian), but in further spiritualizing matter, in participating in the consecration of the world, in sanctifying and supernaturalizing the "real" that has been given to us, by "working together" with God, according to the expression of St. Paul.[27]

Teilhard elaborates at considerable length on this "divinisation of our activities," which are capable of cooperating in the construction of the coming New Jerusalem. In fact, he maintains that "our very passivity and failures are retrievable and useful for the work of God by virtue of the efficacious mystery of the Cross."[28] In this respect Teilhard demonstrates how well he has penetrated the essence of the Christian mystery as unfolded by St. Paul, who never thought of work in terms of individual achievement and its results. In Paul (as also in St. John's Gospel) work embraces "the whole conduct of a man insofar as he falls under the antithesis of good and evil . . . with no distinction between more or less good or evil action . . . and including the hidden motions of the will, whether in relation to God, to the world, or to other men."[29] That is why Paul exhorts the

Philippians[30] not to be afraid to make use of all the things the pagans esteem, as long as these reflect the Divine Plan in terms of the development of human intelligence. For "human intelligence is so important" that "it must be brought into the service of Christ."[31] It is why Paul himself was indifferent to life or death, freedom or imprisonment,[32] as long as all was done with a view to contributing to the creation of a new heaven and a new earth, the final glorification of Jesus. And that is why Teilhard insists on the duty of every Christian to be himself a creator, in some measure, for true Christian asceticism inevitably flows from the requirement of creation to be essentially painful and mortifying. "The mystery of the Cross is present, operating in all creation, in the whole of creation."[33]

This study of St. Paul's teaching on the goods of this world manifests, in a certain sense, the existential nature of Christianity, and consequently the potential appeal of Christianity to the contemporary mind striving for a true reconciliation between God and the world. Paul makes it clear that the Christian life involves an acceptance of the human condition. But this is not carried out in a passive way, for it is more than a mere acceptance. The Christian life looks forward with joy toward a goal, the glorification of Christ and all creatures in Christ. All created things must be prepared for this New Creation by being immersed in and saturated with a love for Christ. Along with St. Paul, Teilhard maintains that this can be done simply by desiring that all actions be motivated and all sufferings be endured through the desire to see God glorified. By pouring over all things the "marvelous substance of good will," both successes and failures, things noble and things base, which by themselves have no direct importance for heaven, become efficacious means whereby the Christian can contribute to the New Creation. The Christian becomes co-creator with God simply by acting "in all things conformably to the will of God."[34]

NOTES

1. Pierre Teilhard de Chardin, *The Divine Milieu* (New York: Harper & Row, 1960), p. 25.
2. Rom. 1:20.
3. 1 Cor. 15:28; cf. also Eph. 1:23.
4. Edgard Haulotte, SJ, *L'Esprit de Yahwe dans 1"Ancien Testament* (in the symposium *L'Homme devant Dieu*, 1964, I, p. 28) on Acts 18:24-29.
5. Henri de Lubac, SJ, *Teilhard de Chardin, The Man and His Meaning* (New York: Hawthorn Books, Inc., 1965), p. 43.
6. F. W. Beare, *A Commentary on the Epistle to the Philippians* (New York: Harper and Row, 1959), p. 115.
7. Rom. 14:14.
8. Tit. 1:15.
9. C. H. Dodd, *The Epistle of Paul to the Romans* (London: Hodder and Stoughton, 1932), p. 216.
10. J. E. Steinmueller and K. Sullivan, "Impure" in *Catholic Biblical Encyclopedia, New Testament* (New York: Joseph F. Wagner, 1959), pp. 325-326. Cf. 1 Tim. 4:5.
11. Dodd, *Epistle of Paul to the Romans*, p. 215; cf. Mark 7:14-23; Acts 10:9-16.
12. Teilhard, *The Divine Milieu*, p. 35.
13. Ph. 3:21; cf. also Eph. 1:23.
14. L. Cerfaux, *Christ in the Theology of St. Paul*, translated by Geoffrey Webb and Adrian Walker (New York: Herder and Herder, 1959), p. 50.
15. Teilhard de Chardin, *The Phenomenon of Man*, translated by Bernard Wall (New York: Harper and Row, 1959), p. 31.
16. Ibid.
17. Ibid., p. 294.
18. T. Agius, SJ, "Le Christ 'Tout on Tout,' " *Revue d'Ascetique et de Mystique*, 2 (1921): 146-161.
19. Rom. 8:22.
20. Claude Tresmontant, *Pierre Teilhard de Chardin, His Thought*, translated by Salvator Attanasio (Baltimore: Helicon Press, 1959), p. 70.
21. Teilhard, *The Phenomenon of Man*, p. 35.
22. Teilhard, *The Divine Milieu*, p. 81.
23. Rom. 8:28.
24. St. John Chrysostom, *The Nicene and Post-Nicene Fathers*, 1st Series, XI, ed. Philip Schaff, Homily 15 (New York: The Christian Literature Company, 1889), p. 452.
25. Teilhard, *The Divine Milieu*, p. 87.
26. Chrysostom, *Nicene and Post-Nicene Fathers*, p. 453.

27. Tresmontant, *Pierre Teilhard de Chardin, His Thought*, pp. 84-85.
28. Teilhard, *The Divine Milieu*, pp. 17-68.
29. George Bertram, "Ergon" in *Theological Dictionary of the New Testament*, ed. Gerhard Kittel, translated by Geoffrey W. Bromiley (Grand Rapids: Wm. B. Eerdmans Publishing Co., 1964), p. 649.
30. Ph. 4:8.
31. Jean Levie, SJ, "Les 'valeurs humanines' dans la theologie de Saint Paul," *Bib* 40 (1959), p. 802.
32. Ph. 1:21-24.
33. Tresmontant, *Pierre Teilhard de Chardin, His Thought*, p. 86.
34. Teilhard, *The Divine Milieu*, p. 22. For pertinent remarks expressed by the Second Vatican Council, cf.: *The Constitution on the Church*, art. 48; *The Constitution on the Sacred Liturgy*, art. 61; *The Constitution on the Church in the Modern World*, art. 10.

TEILHARD AND DANTE
Sister Mariella Gable, OSB

Let us consider man's work. It is both a curse and a blessing. It is a soporific which drugs men into unawareness of the passing of time. He who works with intense interest comes to the end of the day before he knows it has begun. He who toils with heart-absorbing interest speeds the arrival of death. Death surprises him in the midst of consuming interests. Work is also a life-saver. The man to whom retirement is imminent fears like the plague the day he will not go to work. The only alternative to work for him is suffocating boredom. Yet his work harasses him. He longs to leave it for play, agreeing with Tom Sawyer that "work consists of whatever a body is obliged to do; play consists of whatever a body is not obliged to do." And it is in being obliged to stick to continuous effort that many people feel work to be a curse.

In fact, Charles Lamb who hated his work as a clerk in a counting house asked ruefully:

> Who first invented work, and bound the free
> And holiday-rejoicing spirit down . . .
> To that dry drudery of the desk's dead word?

No man escapes entirely the experience of "dry drudgery" in his daily work.

Whichever way we look at it, work presents a problem.

From *American Benedictine Review*, 16 (September, 1965): 341-358. Reprinted by permission of the publisher.

And so it is that we might well listen to one of the greatest modern thinkers when he presents to us a view of work which transfigures it with splendour and beauty. Such a thinker is Teilhard de Chardin.

In the ten years since his death the volume of critical works on him attests to the global interest in his contribution to the thinking of modern man. A dedicated American student[1] of Teilhard noted recently: "The flood of Teilhardian literature undoubtedly will continue to swell." A European scholar[2] noted that "the output of studies on the thought of Teilhard de Chardin shows no sign of slackening." In fact, his thought is like a harvest of wheat purring steadily between two millstones. There are no indifferent readers of Teilhard. There is going on an intensive grinding of his thought between the millstones of the negative thinkers who are disturbed by his discontinuities and the positive thinkers who appreciate the sweep and truth of his cosmic view. I say that this grinding is excellent. For out of this cracking apart of the virgin wheat, the fine white flour of truth will be sifted from the bran of errors and mistakes.

Time, of course, is the judge who holds the golden scales and weighs the value of world visions. The balancing is a long process. We are only in the midst of it. But it is my own guess that the great system of Teilhard de Chardin will make all thinkers of the past kick the beam — even the giants like Plato, Aristotle, and Thomas Aquinas. Nor should this surprise us. For man knows now so much more than he has ever known before. A cosmic view of the universe asks for a Christianity viewed in proportion to that universe.

Teilhard saw with great clarity that we are entering a new age, not in the sense that rationalism or romanticism or the industrial revolution marked new ages. But in the sense that man, who has for over a million years continued in the Neolithic period,[3] is now moving into an entirely different period. Into what?

Into a period which should bring all who see it truly, great joy and great hope. He speaks first of all to those

11

persons who have been troubled by an apparent cleavage between what is true scientifically and what is true in the area of faith. For them he has achieved a synthesis of faith and science. He sees a marvelous unity in which man can no longer be torn between the claims of the spirit and the "seduction" of matter. He is first of all a synthesizer.

He was trained in anthropology, paleontology, geology and various branches of biology. Spending a lifetime in research, he was able to bring the findings of all the sciences to bear upon man's problem in the cosmos. Moreover, as a Jesuit, he had suitable initiation into theology and philosophy. Besides, he was a mystic and a poet. He brought all these competencies to bear at once in whatever problem he attacked.

No longer is it possible to suppose that truth can be attained by keeping disciplines segregated. Truth is one and requires a synthesis of all disciplines. Educators feel the new thrust. The vast changes in curricula throughout the country testify to a new urgency to synthesize learning.

The whole world is being drawn like iron filings to a magnet by Teilhard's system of thought. In the ten years since his death his teaching has spread like wildfire. And the very mention of fire reminds me of one of his pertinent observations:

Let truth appear but once to a single soul, and nothing can ever stop it invading everything and setting everything ablaze.[4]

Perhaps not even a *monitum* from the Holy Office can halt the spread of such fire. We ought to note that the *monitum* of June 30, 1962, which was signed by Sebastianus Masala and which warned that the *Phenomenon of Man* might not appear on the open shelves of seminaries did *not* (and in this it was unlike many other documents from the same office) — it did *not* carry the explicit approval of the reigning pontiff, John XXIII.[5]

In fact, when Pope John was presented with documents condemning Teilhard he refused to sign them. "What," said he, "do you want me to have another Galileo on my hands?" He further declared that he regarded the *monitum* as "very regrettable."[6]

And our reigning pontiff, Paul VI, has described the writings of Teilhard as "indispensable for the thinking of modern man."[7] Indispensable!

Scholars are neither discouraged by the *monitum* nor elated by the admiration of Popes John and Paul. A man of the stature of Teilhard asks simply for the patient analysis and understanding of scholars.

Teilhard's thinking forms a system so perfectly integrated that it is like a carefully wrought design woven into a rug. You pick up the corner of the rug and you lift the whole design. This paper proposes a rather modest lifting of the rug which investigates Teilhard's philosophy of work. It can transfigure our daily toil with immeasurable beauty and radiance.

What has our daily work to do with fame? Fame is the public reputation which follows our work. Whether we like it or not, each of us lives in a circle of fame — limited surely, but valid. One is known for his thoroughness, another for his creative vision, a third for his easy public relations while he shirks productive labor. Another is a slave driver who makes others carry his load. There are as many types of fame as there are individuals in the world.

Teilhard is always a positive thinker. He is concerned with excellence in work and with the aura of fame which surrounds that excellence as certainly as a glow surrounds a candle flame. Fame for him is the good fame of the man who unites making and loving.

Western thought has for centuries troubled itself deeply over the question: Ought man to pursue fame? Milton expressed a typical ambivalence when he spoke of the appetite for fame in "Lycidas." He called it "the last infirmity of noble minds." "Infirmity" suggests a weakness; "noble" suggests strength. Teilhard's thought banishes all such ambivalence.

13

But we must fit his thinking into a long history. Ever since Newman's great book, *The Development of Christian Doctrine* the Church has more and more explicitly accepted the idea that there is a continuous development in man's understanding of truth. There is a perpetual unfolding. To grasp fully the fact of unfolding spares a person many a shock at what he discovers in the past. He sees why things were as they were.

Let us turn back now to Saint Augustine in the fourth and fifth centuries. We find that he took a very sour view of the pursuit of fame. He saw a total cleavage between the City of God and the City of Man. To be concerned with the City of Man, with the material world, was the devil's work. It was, in fact, a sin.[8] But we cannot judge Augustine too harshly. He was the product of his own times. He was greatly influenced by Platonism and Manichaeism.[9]

I believe that Alfred North Whitehead expressed a true evaluation of most of our Western philosophy when he said it was nothing but a collection of footnotes on Plato. But there it has been for centuries — a disturbing dichotomy between matter and spirit. In helping to destroy this dichotomy I believe Teilhard has perhaps made his greatest contribution to humanity and to Christianity. It might be noted here, however, that the destruction of this dichotomy has been assisted by other forces such as the renewed studies in Sacred Scripture and in Hebrew thought.

When we make the long leap between Saint Augustine and the thirteenth century, we find that Saint Thomas took a much more mellow view of the pursuit of fame. In effect he asked that man seek fame under just two conditions: (1) Recognize that your gifts come from God and give God the honor. (2) Use your gifts for the good of mankind.[10] This is basically the position of Teilhard de Chardin. But he deepens and expands this point of view so that the whole pursuit of excellence in work is suffused with a new luminous splendour.

Close to Saint Thomas in time and in vision was Dante.

Dante was nine years old when Saint Thomas died. He was tutored by a pupil of Saint Thomas, and his *Divine Comedy* embodies much of the thinking of Saint Thomas.

I want to make special use of Dante's views on fame in this paper for three reasons:

1. We all know how irritating it is to listen to abstract generalizations if they are not supported by concrete examples. Teilhard de Chardin clearly shows that man has habitually made three wrong answers to the problem of fame and that there is only one right answer. Since Dante illustrated in his *Divine Comedy* all four of the attitudes toward fame which Teilhard presents, I find that I can considerably illuminate this paper, that I can concretize its concepts, by using the examples from Dante.

2. Dante knew by intuition the right attitudes. We have had to wait until Teilhard for a clear statement as to *why* they are right.

3. During this year we are celebrating the seven-hundredth anniversary of the birth of Dante. What more fitting tribute to his memory than to demonstrate how impressively his thinking was just seven hundred years ahead of his time.

Now to the main business of this paper: Teilhard's philosophy of work. I take it mainly from that beautiful little book, *The Divine Milieu*,[11] 139 pages, but pages of pure gold. His other translated works, however, including *The Phenomenon of Man*, *The Future of Man*, and *The Hymn on the Universe* have been consulted. I draw on them for confirming evidence of Teilhard's teaching.

First of all, I want to share with you Teilhard's own clear, honest statement of the dilemma man faces when he looks at fame or at his work in this life: "How can man, who believes in heaven and the Cross, continue to believe seriously in worldly occupation?"[12] This question is simple, clear, honest.

Next, Teilhard tabulates three faulty answers man has made to this dilemma.[13] Finally he presents his own brilliant, heart-warming answer to the problem. I will take up now in order these answers to the problem, both wrong and right, and as I promised you I will conflate them with illustions from the *Divine Comedy*. So let us begin with the three false solutions to the dilemma.

1. In Canto 24 of the "Inferno" Dante describes himself as utterly exhausted by the labors of writing his great poem. He lets the difficulty of climbing a steep embankment in his approach to the thieves symbolize his weariness in work. He says of himself:

The breath was so exhausted from my lungs when I was up that I could no farther; nay I seated me at my first arrival.

Virgil is outraged at this spectacle of one permitting something like personal fatigue to deflect his pursuit of fame. He administers a sharp rebuke to Dante:

Now it behooves thee thus to free thyself from Sloth . . . For sitting on down, or under coverlet, men come not into fame;

And then he adds a general comment on fame which is of capital importance. He says:

And without fame, who so consumes his life, leaves such vestige of himself on earth as smoke in air or foam in water. Therefore rise . . . and act that it may profit thee.

Dante who consistently shows the most profound respect for the opinions of Virgil immediately rose up and "in order to make believe he had more breath than he had, he even went on speaking that he might not seem faint."[14]

Here we have clearly symbolized the man who sees only the material present without any reference to the supernatural. If life without fame is only smoke in air or foam in water, then as Teilhard points out we are dealing with a materialist, who "will dismiss the evangelical counsels to lead what seems to him a complete human life."[15] For Teilhard there is possible no true humanism without the supernatural.

Let us note that this first false solution to the dilemma was offered in Hell.

2. The second false view appears in the "Purgatorio," Canto II. Here on the terrace where pride is punished we meet Oderisi, an artist remembered for his illuminating. At first we see him generously willing to share his honor with a fellow artist, Franco Bolognese — a generosity of which he would not have been capable while alive. But then comes the significant passage — a bitter outburst against the pursuit of fame simply because fame does not last. He cries out:

O empty glory of human powers! How short the time its green endures upon the top . . .

He shows how Cimabue thought to hold the first place in painting and was with great speed superseded by Giotto, how one poet sits for a moment in the public eye as the greatest, only to be shoved aside by a better poet. He concludes that earthly fame is nothing but a breath of wind. He asks dramatically what difference it will make after a thousand years whether any man dies as a child or grows up to do his work. He argues that because the glory of fame is ephemeral one should not work for it.[16]

Teilhard says this viewpoint is typical of the Christian who will force himself to concentrate "on purely religious objects only"[17] — to the exclusion of the largest possible number of worldly objects. This is a kind of Platonism.

3. Teilhard singles out the undecided as representative of the third wrong way to meet the dilemma. The undecided are the fence-straddlers who cannot make up their minds as to the claims of matter and spirit. Dante had a special horror for these trimmers. He expressed this horror by locating them *outside* Hell, for if he had placed them *in* Hell the devils would have lorded it over them; the devils at least made up their minds.[18] "Because you are neither hot nor cold I will vomit you out of my mouth."[19] Dante further suggests the utter damnation of the trimmers by keeping them anonymous. Nowhere else in the "Inferno" does he

refuse to name individuals. His disgust for the spirit of those who cannot decide is total, furious, and frightening.

Teilhard de Chardin is also hard on the undecided. He finds them "imperfect in their own eye and insincere in the eyes of men." They are to be deplored because they have "become resigned to living a double life."[20]

4. Now we come to the only appropriate solution to the dilemma, which, as we have seen, postulates some opposition between matter and spirit. Teilhard once and for all rules out this dichotomy by showing that our problem is not either-or, not either matter or spirit. It is both-and, both matter and spirit. Both matter and spirit united inseparably deserve our total dedication. Why? As Teilhard saw it, Christ is present in matter the way light irradiates a crystal.[21] The light is not the crystal and the crystal is not the light. But they are united in the way that light irradiates a crystal — "without immixture, without confusion."[22] His critics like to accuse Teilhard of being a pantheist; repeatedly Teilhard denies that he teaches pantheism.[23]

Through a lifetime of thinking Teilhard arrived at his Christology, based solidly on Saint Paul and Saint John. He began with the presence of Christ in the Holy Eucharist.

In the *Hymn of the Universe* Teilhard includes three beautiful little *contes* in which as early as 1916 he made his thinking clear. In a mystical vision he saw the host at exposition expanding to embrace the whole cosmos. Christ's presence "overran everything." "At the same time everything, though drowned in this whiteness, preserved its own proper shape . . . for the whiteness did not efface the features or change the nature of anything, but penetrated objects at the core of their being. . . . It was as though a milky brightness were illuminating the universe from within and everything were fashioned of the same kind of translucent flesh. . . . So through the mysterious expansion of the host, the whole world had become incandescent, had become itself like a single giant host."[24]

As to the relationship between the Eucharist and Christ's

presence in the whole universe Teilhard asks the following:

> But how can we avoid going further and believing that the sacramental action of Christ, precisely because it sanctifies matter, extends its influence, beyond the pure supernatural, over all that makes up the internal and external ambiance of the faithful, that is to say that it sets its mark upon everything which we call 'our Providence?'

> If this is the case, then we find ourselves (by simply having followed the 'extension' of the Eucharist) plunged once again precisely into our divine milieu. . . . Christ reveals Himself in each reality around us, and shines like an ultimate determinant, like a center, one might almost say like a universal element. As our humanity assimilates the material world, and the Host assimilates our humanity, the eucharistic transformation goes beyond and completes the transubstantiation of the bread on the altar. Step by step it irresistibly invades the universe. . . .

> In a secondary and generalized sense but in a true sense the sacramental Species are formed by the totality of the world, and the duration of creation is needed for its consecration.[25]

Though such a passage is somewhat unsatisfying because it depends upon a rhetorical question and assertion, we shall see in a moment how much stronger becomes his argument when he invokes the evidence of St. Paul. But first let us note this. Teilhard recognized that his doctrine of the omnipresence of Christ was different from "the unusual speculation which is current concerning the presence of God," and that this difference lay in the idea that "the presence of God reaches the elements of the world only through and in the Body of Christ."[26]

This doctrine of the omnipresence of Christ was of capital importance to the whole system of Teilhard de Chardin. Of the evolution of the universe from the beginning of matter to our own time he had what seems to be persuasive evidence. By an extremely probable extrapolation he sees that this same evolution, which has as its aim the emergence of man, is destined to continue in the direction of the ever more spiritual development of mankind. This continued evolution of the material universe he calls cosmogenesis. He also sees that this cosmogenesis is bringing with it a new era of the unification and convergence of mankind in love and compassion.[27] He cannot believe that this ultimate in the cosmogenesis is separtate from or different from the Christogenesis of the universe — in which all men will be one in Christ.

Teilhard is particularly eloquent in asserting the oneness of cosmogenesis and Christogenesis. He says, for instance, "The world can no more have two summits than a circumference can have two centers."[28] And again he declares, "To build the City of Man is already to build the City of God."[29]

Teilhard saw that the development of science asked for an interpretation of Christ concomitant with the extensiveness of the cosmos. He asked with great concern: "Is the Christ of the Gospel imagined and loved within the dimensions of the Mediterranean world capable of still embracing and still forming the center of our prodigiously expanded universe? Is the world not in the process of becoming more vast, more close, more dazzling than Jehovah? Will it not burst our religion asunder — eclipse our God?"[30] It was for the millions of men who see the development of science as a threat to faith that he made the supreme effort to bring together science and faith. The culmination of this union Teilhard names the Omega point.

Now this Omega on the scientific level is an extrapolation reached only from phenomena. It is an assumption and a conjecture which cannot provide the necessary guarantee of cosmogenesis.[31] Teilhard felt the need to bridge the gap. He needed to show how the Christ of revelation may be identified with the Omega of evolution. In order to bridge this gap he drew on Scripture, specifically on Saint John and Saint Paul. He repeatedly made use of what Dr. Christopher Mooney calls the three cosmic texts of Saint Paul. These texts, according to Mooney, have "received relatively little attention and almost no development since the time of the Greek Fathers . . . it is only in recent years that the so-called cosmic texts have emerged as subjects of discussion and debate."[32] I might remark here that Father Christopher F. Mooney has explored in complex detail Teilhard's whole treatment of the Body of Christ in *Theological Studies*.[33] This study is of special value since Father Mooney as a member of the *Institut Catholique* of Paris has been able to consult sources not available to American scholars. He saw that the question with which we have to deal here is simply this: "To what extent can Paul be said to extend the physical relationship between Christ and mankind to the whole creation, including therefore all that is material?"[34]

The sources on which one relies for an answer are extremely limited. They are the three cosmic texts of Saint Paul: Rom. 8:19-23, Col. 1:15-20, and Eph. 1:9-10, 22-23.[35] These passages have usually not been approached by the exegetes with the precise aim of determining Christ's relationship to the material world. But there is a new direction now being taken by a number of authors who are aware that they must discover what Paul might have meant about the presence of Christ in the material universe.

Father Mooney gives an interpretation favorable to Teilhard's view. He shows how in Col. 1:15-20 Paul "goes back to the pre-existence of Christ in the Father, in whose image (*eikon*) He is the source as well as the instrument and final end of creation. The Incarnation, crowned by the triumph of the Resurrection, is seen as placing the human nature of Christ at the head not only of the whole human race but also of the entire created universe."[36] Father Mooney's concluding analysis lends superb support to the use Teilhard makes of this passage of Saint Paul. He says:

For many people today the "Plenitude" of Christ in this extraordinary text, His Pleroma, represents in Paul's mind the extension of Christ's work of redemption to the whole cosmos, the whole of creation.... Christ is God, and through his work of redemption He unites himself not only to redeemed humanity ... but also to the whole of the cosmos which is humanity's dwelling place."[37]

The limitations of this paper do not permit me to examine the other cosmic texts of Saint Paul. We should note, however, that exegetes are not at one in their interpretation of Saint Paul and that interpreting the cosmic texts is still an open question to theologians.[38]

But for Teilhard, Christ's physical presence in the universe was a basic tenet. He believed with overwhelming faith that "God is in some sort at the tip of my pen, my spade, my brush, my needle."[39] By doing my work, whatever it is, I become a co-creator with Christ in the continued evolution of the cosmos toward the Pleroma. What I do does not matter. If I know that I am doing Christ's work I must enter into it with creative joy and enthusiasm. Sometimes the humblest labor undertaken with total dedication can lead to the most astonishing discoveries.

I think, for instance, of a novice at Königskloster in 1843. It was young Gregor Mendel, an Augustinian monk who later became Abbot and who never could pass the examination for the teaching profession. As a novice he asked for permission to plant tall peas and dwarf peas in the monastery garden. He cross-fertilized them and kept accurate records. Later he published his findings in a scientific journal to which the world paid not the slightest attention. Not until thirty-four years after his death did scientists awaken to the great importance of his discovery of Mendel's Law, which "laid the foundation for the science of genetics."[40]

But it does not matter whether you are a Father Gregor Mendel or an ordinary botany student entering with the fullness of joyful enthusiasm into the problems of taxonomy.

I think of Maria Montessori trained as a teacher. She used to look at little boys and girls in rows in a classroom and think they were like dead butterflies mounted on a bulletin board. She thought they deserved a better education. Then she received her first assignment: to teach a group of mentally retarded children. To her this was a great blow. But she met the challenge with such creative energy that her defective children passed the state examinations in reading and writing for normal children.[41] Now, thanks to her, educators are widely introducing something we call the Montessori method. But in the same class with her is the young religious sister who enters into her practice teaching with total creative zest and enthusiasm. Christ's evolutionary plan for the cosmos is served well both by those whose excellence wins for them great fame as well as by those who win small fame.

The Christian worker always says "yes" if at all possible when he is asked to perform a task. That he is placed in a situation where his gifts are asked for is indication that it is the will of God that he perform what he can.

The Christian worker never indulges in discontent with present circumstances. He does not dream of a different place, a different superior, of different circumstances. This moment, this work, this spot — here and now — these are God's will for me and deserve my most creative effort. There were those who advised Teilhard to become a secularized priest since his order exiled him from France for nearly a lifetime in China. But this he would never consider. For him the Jesuit order was the "Divine Milieu" and he would not entertain the thought of leaving it. In fact, "Divine Milieu" means simply the presence of Christ in the universe.

Now what about the cross? No Christian can neglect it. It has, however, often been grievously misunderstood. Being co-creators with Christ requires of us unflagging effort. Fatigue, boredom, and weariness are the ordinary price one has to pay for a job well done. Effort means carrying our cross with painful perseverance. It means renouncing personal comfort and slothful ease. If we are engaged in *creative* effort our days are dogged by continual rejection of trial efforts and scores of new beginnings.[42]

Finally, there is the whole important area of diminishment.[43] God has many ways of requiring the diminishment of the individual: personal illness, or the envious obstruction of our work by the malice or the misunderstanding of others, or the approach of old age — a diminishment no one can escape. The list could be extended indefinitely. All of them the co-creator with Christ bears in perfect peace of soul. But no man has the right to diminish himself for the sake of diminishing himself.[44] He continues to do his utmost. Homer and Milton were both blind. Beethoven was deaf. Not one of them discontinued his creative work because of his personal diminishment. The co-creator with Christ is forever at peace. He is united to God not only by intention but also by the attention he gives to every moment of his work. This attention becomes a kind of adoration. He is forever spared the hardest cross of all to bear, the pain of being divided between the material and the spiritual world.

Dante saw all this very clearly. In the opening canto of the "Paradiso" Dante prays to Christ, under the name of Apollo, begging for the grace to write of Heaven well.[45] He explains to Christ that if he can communicate only a shadow of Heaven, then he will come to the laurel tree to be crowned by Christ for success.[46] Then he bursts out with a bitter complaint against those who do not aim at fame. In a sense he argues with Christ in favor of those who do their utmost. He says:

So few times, Father, is there gathered of it (the laurel of fame) for triumph of Caesar or of poet — fault and shame of human wills — that the Penian frond should bring forth gladness in the joyous Delphic deity when it sets *any* athirst for itself.[47]

Notice that he mentioned both politics and poetry as fields in which man should be seeking fame. He shows how important it is to aim for the highest since "one great man inspires another to greatness."[48] And on the basis of this argument he begs for personal success.

Dante comes much more directly to the problem of fame, however, in Canto 17 of the "Paradiso," the canto in which he meets Cacciaguida, his own great, great grandfather, who is both a martyr and a saint. First of all the old man prophesies with great clarity Dante's exile from Florence and how he shall have to leave behind him all his dear ones as well as to suffer the continued humiliation of living among strangers.

24

Thou shalt make trial how salt doth taste another's bread
And how hard the path to descend and mount another's stair.[49]

This is Dante's diminishment. He accepts it without complaint. But his poem, the *Divine Comedy,* his life work, that is another matter. How can he save that for mankind? How can he win fame? He has a specific problem. He has been shown things in his journey through Hell and Purgatory which people will not like to hear: perhaps his vision of the popes in Hell suffering for simony. Dante says that if he tells his whole vision of the next life accurately, it will have a "strong-bitter flavor to many."[50] And he knows precisely what the cost to him will be if he does not tell the whole truth as it has been revealed to him. He says:

If to truth I am a shrinking friend, I fear to be forgotten in ages yet unborn.[51]

In other words he will miss winning fame.

His saintly grandfather puts his heart at rest:

Every lie set aside. Make thy entire vision manifest, and let them scratch where is the scab.[52]

The great artist communicates truth as he knows it and he who dares to be true dares to be great. Teilhard thought that our own age needs men who are willing to die for truth. He himself suffered greatly for truth. In fact, both Teilhard and Dante were exiles, Dante for political reasons and Teilhard because he would not say less than the truth as he saw it about evolution.

Dante even provided a very special heaven in the planet of Mercury for those "good spirits who were active that honor and that fame might come to them."[53] Intuitively he knew he had the truth. But we had to wait for Teilhard to explain *how* it is true, how we are by our work co-creators with Christ. However, it might be pointed out that now there are a goodly number of progressive theologians, men like Karl Rahner, Delubac, and Mersch who are bringing the force of their thinking to bear in the same direction.

Let us take a quick glance at that heaven which Dante reserved for "those good spirits who were active that honor and that fame might come to them." Side by side in this heaven of Mercury he featured two things:

1. The success of a Roman Emperor, Justinian, who codified Roman Law. He is the exemplar of the man who has worthily sought fame.[54]

2. Immediately following the account of Justinian's fame comes the "chief theological discourse in the Paradiso."[55] It is on the Incarnation and the Redemption — as if Dante had felt with Teilhard de Chardin the need to keep these two concepts together — the concept of excellence in work and the concept of the Incarnation.[56]

Thus far we have noted only correspondences between Dante and Teilhard. They are significant and impressive. Let us look at one difference — a difference perhaps more eloquent than all the correspondences. It underlines the extent to which Teilhard is a spiritual pioneer. Dante's Heaven of Mercury is one of the lowest of Dante's ten heavens. In fact, it is the second lowest. In the final construct of the poem Dante makes it clear that the first three heavens are for those souls who had practiced in an imperfect way the virtues of faith, hope, and charity. In the Heaven of Mercury are those who practiced an imperfect hope. Hope of fame, then, becomes an imperfect thing as compared to hope of Heaven which is a perfect thing. Dante further symbolizes this imperfection by letting a cone-shaped shadow of the earth fall on these first three heavens.

To Teilhard such a concept would be totally deplorable. To him, man as co-creator with Christ in doing his work well is practicing the highest type of conformity to God's will. He even went so far as to point out that when man once grasps the full import of his work as co-creator with Christ "there would be little to separate life in the cloister from life in the world."[57]

In other words our labor properly understood makes all life religious life. For Benedictines this idea is of profound importance, for we live by the mystique that work is prayer.

It is this religious concept which Teilhard commends to all of us. One works hard, exercises unflagging effort to make one's work excellent, not because one cares about the recognition of others, but because excellence is holy. Excellence is beautiful. Excellence is apocalyptic. Our work assists in moving the cosmogenesis and Christogenesis of this world more swiftly toward the Pleroma, that fullness in Christ which gives meaning to all effort. Teilhard himself recaptured the joyous expectation of the Pleroma which animated the Church in the days of Saint Paul. We are moving with tremendous speed out of noosphere, an envelope of knowing, into the Christosphere, an envelope of loving, in which all men will be united.[58] In Christ present in the material universe "we live and move and have our being."[59] We must learn not to resist technological progress but to promote it, for it is part of a magnificent total plan for the consummation of the world. On both the scientific and Christological level Teilhard's system "allows technological man to feel that henceforth he is on the road (planned by God) to Christianity, and not simply the servant of a dehumanized, accursed world: thus the modern world of technology acquires value from the invisible world."[60]

"The whole of nature has been groaning until now in an agony of birth."[61] All workers are co-creators with Christ in assisting at this birth, this becoming, this Pleroma. This is a view of mankind which "substitutes progressive optimism for static pessimism."[62] We have now a Christ-centered cosmos in which the heart rises joyously and creatively to the opportunity to spend a life-time of effort in being co-creators with Christ.

NOTES

1. Robert T. Francoeur, S.J., "Teilhard de Chardin," *Jubilee*, 14 (July, 1965): 39.

2. William Donnelly, S.J., "Teilhardian Vision," *The Month,* 33 (April, 1965): 249.

3. Claude Cuénot, *Teilhard de Chardin: A Biographical Study* (Baltimore: Helicon, 1965), p. 109.

4. Ibid., 373. From *Le Critique,* page not given.

5. Donald J. Campion, S.J., "Tired of Chardin," *America,* CXIII (May 15, 1965), 697.

6. Quoted in a letter by Robert T. Francoeur, S.J., to Sister Jeremy Hall, O.S.B., spring 1964. I asked Father Francoeur if this quotation could be verified. He assured me that it was most certainly true but that the ecclesiastic who reported it prefers to remain anonymous.

7. Francoeur, p. 36. Father Francoeur says: As Pope Paul remarked to a high ranking member of the hierarchy last spring, "Le Pere Teilhard est indispensable i notre temps, son apologetique est necessaire!"

8. Mortimer J. Adler and William Gorman, editors, *The Great Ideas: A Syntopicon of Great Books of the Western World,* I, p. 734.

9. Maurice B. McNamee, S.J., *Honor and the Epic Hero* (New York: Holt, Rinehart & Winston, 1960), p. 120.

10. Ibid., p. 125.

11. Pierre Teilhard de Chardin, *The Divine Milieu: An Essay on the Interior Life* (New York: Harper & Row, 1960).

12. Ibid., p. 19.

13. Ibid.

14. Dante Alighieri, *La Divina Commedia.* The Italian edited by H. Oelsner, English translation by J. A. Carlyle, Thomas Okay, and P. H. Wicksteed.

15. Teilhard, *The Divine Milieu,* p. 20.

16. Dante, "Purgatorio" II, lines 91-106.

17. Teilhard, *The Divine Milieu,* p. 20.

18. Dante, "Inferno" 3, line 42.

19. Apocalypse 3:16.

20. Teilhard, *The Divine Milieu,* pp. 20-21.

21. Ibid., p. 15.

22. Ibid., p. 23.

23. Ibid., p. 93. Teilhard says, ". . . the sojourner in the divine milieu is not a pantheist. At first sight, perhaps, the depths of the divine which St. Paul reveals to us may seem to resemble the fascinating domain unfolded before our eyes by monistic philosophies or religions. In fact, they are very different. . . ." The passage develops the difference between pantheism and Teilhard's thought.

24. Pierre Teilhard de Chardin, *Hymn of the Universe* (New York: Harper & Ros, 1965), p. 48.

25. Teilhard, *The Divine Milieu,* pp. 104-105.

26. Teilhard, *Mon Univers* (1924), pp. 24-25, 26, 49 note 1. Quoted in Christopher F. Mooney, S.J., "The Body of Christ in the Writings of Teilhard de Chardin," *Theological Studies*, 25 (December, 1964): 587.

27. Pierre Teilhard de Chardin, *The Future of Man*, trans. from the French by Norman Denny (New York: Harper & Row, 1964), p. 224.

28. Teilhard, *The Divine Milieu*, p. 137.

29. Cuénot, p. 107.

30. Teilhard, *The Divine Milieu*, p. 14.

31. Mooney, "The Body of Christ in the Writings of Teilhard de Chardin," p. 577.

32. Ibid., p. 595.

33. See note 26.

34. Mooney, "The Body of Christ in the Writings of Teilhard de Chardin," p. 601.

35. The three cosmic passages are as follows, the translation taken from the Revised Standard Version (Catholic Edition) of the New Testament: Rom. 8:19-23. "For the creation waits with eager longing for the revealing of the sons of God; for the creation was subjected to futility, not of its own will but by the will of him who subjected it in hope; because the creation itself will be set free from its bondage to decay and obtain the glorious liberty of the children of God. We know that the whole creation has been groaning in travail together until now; and not only the creation, but we ourselves, who have the first fruits of the Spirit, groan inwardly as we wait for adoption as sons, the redemption of our bodies."

Col. 1:15-20. "He is the image of the invisible God, the first-born of all creation; for in him all things were created, in heaven and on earth, visible and invisible, whether thrones or dominations or principalities or authorities — all things were created through him and for him. He is before all things, and in him all things hold together. He is the head of the body, the church, he is the beginning, the first-born from the dead, that in everything he might be pre-eminent. For in him all the fulness of God was pleased to dwell, and through him to reconcile to himself all things, whether on earth or in heaven, making peace by the blood of his cross."

Eph. 1:9-10, 22-23. "For he has made known to us in all wisdom and insight the mystery of his will, according to his purpose which he set forth in Christ as a plan for the fulness of time, to unite all things in him, things in heaven and things on earth, and he has put all things under his feet and has made him the head over all things for the church, which is his body, the fulness of him who fills all in all."

29

36. Mooney, "The Body of Christ in the Writings of Teilhard de Chardin," p. 603.
37. Ibid., p. 604.
38. Ibid., p. 606.
39. Teilhard, *The Divine Milieu*, p. 33.
40. Gregor Johann Mendell (1822-1884), *Encyclopedia Brittanica*, 1965, XV, pp. 146-7.
41. Maria Montessori (1870-1952), Ibid., p. 786.
42. Teilhard, *The Divine Milieu*, p. 41.
43. Ibid., pp. 53-4.
44. Ibid., p. 73.
45. Dante, "Paradiso," i, line 13.
46. Ibid., line 25.
47. Ibid., lines 28-34.
48. Ibid., line 34.
49. Ibid., Canto 17, lines 58-60.
50. Ibid., line 117.
51. Ibid., lines 118-120.
52. Ibid., lines 127-129.
53. Ibid., Canto 6, lines 112-114.
54. Ibid., Canto 6 entire.
55. Introductory paragraph to "Paradiso" Canto 6 in Carlyle-Okey-Wicksteed translation. See note 15.
56. To the traditionalist this juxtaposition of the two concepts is just another example of Dante's teaching on Church and State. Justinian represents the State and the Incarnation forms the heart of the Church. I believe this interpretation is valid, but that Dante's whole concept of Church and State takes on new depth and meaning from the implications of the teaching of Teilhard de Chardin.
57. Teilhard, *The Divine Milieu*, p. 37.
58. Pierre Teilhard de Chardin, *The Phenomenon of Man*, with an Introduction by Sir Julian Huxley, (New York: Harper & Row, 1959), Bk IV, Chap. II: "Beyond the Collective: The Hyper-Personal," pp. 254-272.
59. Acts 17:28.
60. Cuénot, p. 404.
61. Rom. 8:22.
62. Cuénot, p. 399. This statement is part of a remarkable summary of Teilhard's achievement: "By a master stroke Teilhard, by reconciling twentieth-century man with himself, reconciles Christianity with evolutionist science, substitutes progressive optimism for static pessimism, and finds again a treasure buried since the days of St. Paul and St. Irenaeus, 'the meaning of the cosmic component of salvation,' of Christ, in whom all things are taken up."

TENNYSON AND TEILHARD
Eugene R. August

"*In Memoriam* can, I think, justly be called a religious poem ... because of the quality of its doubt. Its faith is a poor thing, but its doubt is a very intense experience."[1] Thus, in the early years of this century did T. S. Eliot state the case for reading *In Memoriam* as a poem of doubt veneered by an inadequate faith. By calling the poem's faith "a poor thing," Eliot apparently meant two things. First, the faith was not deeply professed by Tennyson himself: "Tennyson's contemporaries ... may have been taken in by it," Eliot says, "but I don't think that Tennyson himself was, quite: his feelings were more honest than his mind" (p. 187). And, second, the faith was poor because serious thinking men today could see through its contradictions. "The hope of immortality," Eliot argues, "is confused (typically of the period) with the hope of the gradual and steady improvement of this world" (p. 186). Eliot's two points are related: the poem's faith is a poor thing because Tennyson was half aware that he had compromised his religious beliefs with the Philistine doctrine of material progress.

In one form or another these objections to the poem's faith have been leveled at *In Memoriam* since its publication. As early as the 1850's Matthew Arnold was reading it as a poem of doubt. In "The Scholar-Gipsy" (ll. 182-186), he

---

Reprinted by permission of the Modern Language Association from *PMLA*, 84 (March, 1969): 217-226.

drew a gloomy portrait of the author of *In Memoriam:*

> . . . and amongst us one,
> Who most has suffered, takes dejectedly
> His seat upon the intellectual throne;
> And all his store of sad experience he
> Lays bare of wretched days.[2]

For Arnold, the poem's faith was too poor a thing to cure the strange disease of modern life.

In the twentieth century, Harold Nicolson argued that the real *In Memoriam* was to be found in the original, heart-wrung elegies lamenting Hallam's death, and not in "the theological treatise on the conflict between faith and doubt, religion and dogma, belief and science."[3] Hoping to make Tennyson palatable to a recalcitrant generation, Nicolson directed attention away from the "outdated" faith to the poignant lament for Hallam. He urged the reader to "forget the delicate Laureate of a cautious age; the shallow thought, the vacant compromise. . . . Let us recall only the low booming of the North Sea upon the dunes; . . . the cold, the half-light, and the gloom" (p. 306).

Later critics have not been kinder to the poem's faith.[4] E. D. H. Johnson feels that Tennyson's alienated vision is falsified by *In Memoriam*'s triumphant conclusion. Only half aware of the inadequate compromise he had effected, Tennyson "chooses to believe," according to Johnson, that he has "brought his poetry into tune with the spirit of the age."[5] Robin Mayhead, hostile to Tennyson as an artist, apparently regards it as a historical curiosity that anyone took the poem's faith seriously.[6] Even a sympathetic critic like Valerie Pitt winces over "Tennyson's half-comprehending and totally unconvincing reconciliation of the religious and the scientific conceptions of the universe."[7] Summing up the case against the poem's faith, George O. Marshall in the recent *Tennyson Handbook* states that *In Memoriam* no longer serves its purpose "of bolstering faith in the meaning of life."[8] Quoting Eliot on the quality of the poem's doubt,

Marshall concludes: "And so it seems to the twentieth century, which regards Tennyson as much more pessimistic than his contemporaries thought him to be" (p. 124). In short, the poem's faith is a poor thing.

This alleged inadequacy in the poem should be faced squarely. Tennyson intended the poem to portray a convincing resolution of doubt by faith. He called *In Memoriam* "the way of a soul," which was supposed to portray not only "the different moods of sorrow" but also "my conviction that fear, doubts, and suffering will find answer and relief only through Faith in a God of Love."[9] If the poem's faith is a poor thing, then *In Memoriam* is badly flawed because it does not achieve the resolution that it is so obviously trying for. Moreover, its worth is diminished if present-day readers can discover nothing but antiquarian value in its faith. The faiths embodied in *The Divine Comedy* and *Paradise Lost* have relevance to modern man (as Dorothy L. Sayers and C. S. Lewis have so ably demonstrated),[10] and clearly their value to us is hereby enhanced. About *In Memoriam,* therefore, the question should be honestly raised: can twentieth-century men who have lived through two world wars, Auschwitz and Hiroshima, Korea and Vietnam, still take seriously Tennyson's belief in progress and his hope of immortality? The question is not whether all men can share Tennyson's faith (for that is clearly impossible), but whether liberally minded men can accord it respect. Or, must modern readers reject the faith of *In Memoriam* as a poor thing, a shabby compromise between traditional religion and a belief in material progress?

This article proposes that the faith of *In Memoriam* is anything but a Victorian curiosity. On the contrary, it foreshadows a recent and dynamic strand of twentieth-century religious thought, perhaps best expounded by the priest-paleontologist Pierre Teilhard de Chardin. Linking Tennyson's name with Teilhard's will no doubt seem ludicrous to many. What can "the stupidest of English poets" have in common with "the Aquinas of the Atomic Age"? And yet, just as surely as Tennyson anticipated the religious doubt that Charles Darwin was to precipitate upon the Victorian era, so also did he anticipate the shape of the faith that Teilhard was to forge in the twentieth century from his synthesis of religion and science. Moreover, the way in which Tennyson prepares the reader to accept the poem's faith is similar to that used by Teilhard in his masterwork *The Phenomenon of Man.* In both thought and strategy, then, there is a bond between the two men.[11]

Viewed in the light of Teilhard's work, the faith of *In Memoriam* can be seen more clearly for what it is — a faith so radically modern that many critics, thinking in more conventional terms, have mistakenly dismissed it as a poor thing.

II

Putting *In Memoriam* side by side with *The Phenomenon of Man* reveals their agreement on three crucial points: the importance of seeing the human phenomenon in the light of recent scientific knowledge, the nature of doubt that afflicts modern man, and the shape that belief must take if man is to survive. Often, what Tennyson as poet portrays in particular and personal terms is what Teilhard as scientist discusses in general ones. Finally, both works attempt in a similar way to awaken the reader's assent to their new vision of man.

In Memoriam is one of the few poems in which an attempt is made to see man as a biological phenomenon with a past, present, and future. Teilhard, at the start of *The Phenomenon of Man,* stresses the need for men to base their thought on the realities of the human phenomenon; either man will see, Teilhard says, or he will perish.[12] Tennyson, studying works like the *Principles of Geology,* the *Vestiges of Creation,* and the *Preliminary Discourse on the Study of Natural Philosophy,* was making this effort to see the phenomenon of man as contemporary science revealed it. In *In Memoriam* he is acutely aware that man's biological past stretches backward into the dim origins of life, that this planet is but a tiny globe spinning through an immeasurable universe, and that time and space are not comfortably tailored to man's measure:

> They say,
> The solid earth whereon we tread
>
> In tracts of fluent heat began,
>   And grew to seeming-random forms
>   The seeming prey of cyclic storms,
> Till at the last arose the man.[13]

Tennyson, of course, does not have Teilhard's more advanced, firsthand scientific knowledge. Like most Victorians, he "thinks of science as entirely inductive and empirical; he has no inkling of the extent to which later science will be deductive and conceptual."[14] He is uncertain, moreover, how the different species originated (Darwin's famous study was not published until nine years after the poem was), and he holds a somewhat confused concept of embryonic development.[15] These vagaries, however, never eclipse the essential accuracy of his scientific view. Tennyson, as A. C. Bradley noted in 1929, is the only poet "to whose habitual way of seeing, imagining, or thinking, it makes any real difference that Laplace, or for that matter Copernicus, ever lived."[16] When Tennyson asks us *In Memoriam* to "contemplate all this work of Time" (CXVII.1), he is urging only what he himself has done throughout the poem.

The immediate result of this effort to see is a paralyzing doubt about the meaning of human existence. This doubt, recorded so vividly in *In Memoriam,* is the same malady described in *The Phenomenon of Man.* Teilhard points out that anxiety is the price modern man pays for seeing the world anew: "For our mind to adjust itself to lines and horizons enlarged beyond measure, it must renounce the comfort of familiar narrowness" (p. 225). To his credit, Tennyson had renounced the familiar narrowness of conventional concepts of the universe. But the result of this daring is evident in *In Memoriam*'s terrifying fear that man is an insignificant event in a purposeless universe. Teilhard calls this fear "the malady of space-time." "The whole psychology of modern disquiet," he says, "is linked with the sudden confrontation with space-time . . . . In the first and most widespread degree, the 'malady of space-time' manifests itself as a rule by a feeling of futility, of being crushed by the enormities of the cosmos" (pp. 225-226). There could be no better description of the doubt pervading *In Memoriam,* especially Sections LV and LVI where Tennyson desperately wonders: "Are God and Nature then at strife, / That Nature lends such evil dreams?" (LV.5-6).[17] Nature implies that a man's individual existence is negligible. Worse, Nature has wiped out "a thousand types," implying that the whole human species is a foredoomed joke. In this absurd world, man — who can perceive the awful absurdity — is an evolutionary monstrosity:

> Dragons of the prime,
> That tare each other in their slime,
> Were mellow music match'd with him.
> (LVI.22-24)

Faced with such a horror, Tennyson can only exclaim: "O life as futile, then, as frail!" (LVI.25).

It is a mistake to argue that "despite numerous references to scientific ideas, despite *[Tennyson's]* anxiety to keep up to date with scientific progress, science has little or nothing to do with his best and most characteristic poetry."[18] On the contrary, the much-admired quality of doubt in *In Memoriam* has everything to do with science. Tennyson's doubt springs directly from "living" a boundless universe. "Which of us," Teilhard asks, "has ever in his life really had the courage to look squarely at and try to 'live' a universe formed of galaxies whose distance apart runs into hundreds of thousands of light years? Which of us, having tried, has not emerged from the ordeal shaken in one or other of his beliefs?" (p. 226). Tennyson tried to live the kind of universe Teilhard describes. Once, responding to his brother's fears about attending a dinner party, Tennyson remarked, "Fred, think of Herschel's great starpatches, and you will soon get over all that" *(Memoir,* I, 20). In "The Two Voices," Tennyson's small, still voice of Despair constantly alludes to man's insignificance in a boundless universe.[19] Early in *In Memoriam,* Sorrow voices the worst fear of the space-time malady when she whispers that the stars "blindly run" (III.5). Clearly "one or other" of Tennyson's beliefs had been badly shaken. The gloom of the lonely Lincolnshire poet, so rightly admired by Nicolson and others, stems partly from Tennyson's attempt to look squarely at and live Herschel's great star-patches.

The doubt of *In Memoriam,* of course, had particular as well as cosmic origins, and here again there is a parallel with Teilhard's experience. Arthur Hallam's apparently senseless death precipitated Tennyson's spiritual crisis by painfully straining the poet's belief in spiritual evolution. How could Nature be aiming at the evolution of finer men like Hallam when it wantonly destroyed the living Hallam in his youth? *In Memoriam* is largely the way of a soul trying to cope with the meaning of this death. This kind of experience was well known to Teilhard, and his work is at least partly a response to death's challenge to faith. When his friend Davidson Black died suddenly in 1934, Teilhard wrote:

Today I am deeply aware of the call to rescue the world from the blackness of its materialism. You already know that Dr. Black has died. The apparent absurdity of that untimely end, the noble but blind acceptance of this tragedy by his friends here, the complete absence of "light" on the poor body lying in that cold room at the Peiping Union Medical College — all these lent a leaden quality to my sadness, and revolted my spirit.

Either there is an escape from death — somewhere — for an individual's thought, for his self-consciousness, or else the world is a hideous mistake. And if it is, then there is no use in our going on. But, since the uselessness of going on is an idea intolerable to everyone, the alternative must be to *believe.* To awaken this belief shall be, now more than ever, my task. I swear it. I have sworn it on the mortal remains of Davy, that more than brother of mine.[20]

In another letter, the priest wrote: "I miss Black very much. Missing him is like a shadow, or an emptiness that I carry wherever I go."[21] The similarity to the sorrow of *In Memoriam* should be obvious, for Tennyson also was aware that if there was not some escape from death, then the world is a hideous mistake.

Both Tennyson and Teilhard agree that if men cannot believe in survival after death, then human life, activity, and the entire evolutionary process will grind to a halt. If there is no chance that "life shall live for evermore," Tennyson says, then "earth is darkness at the core, / And dust and ashes all that is" (XXXIV.3-4). Teilhard argues that "the radical defect in all forms of belief in progress, as they are expressed in positivist credos, is that they do not definitely eliminate death" (pp. 269-270). Attacking those "positivist and critical" thinkers who say "that the new generation, less ingenuous than their elders, no longer believes in a future and in a perfecting of the world," Teilhard asks: "Has it even occurred to those who write and repeat these things that, if they were right, all spiritual movement on earth would be virtually brought to a stop? . . . Even on stacks of material energy, even under the spur of immediate fear or desire, *without the taste for life,* mankind would soon stop inventing and constructing for a work it knew to be doomed in advance" (pp. 230-231). As a basic wage for human effort, man needs to know, first, that there can be a "suitable outcome" to evolution and, second, that "there is for us, in the future, under some form or another, at least collective, not only continuation but also *survival*" (pp. 232-233). Without such a belief in progress and survival, man is doomed. "If progress is a myth," Teilhard writes, "that is to say, if faced by the work involved we can say: 'What's the good of it all?' our efforts will flag. With that the whole of evolution will come to a halt — because we are evolution" (p. 231).

This paralysis of human effort is exactly what afflicts Tennyson in *In Memoriam.* As usual, the poet depicts in personal terms what the scientist has discussed in general ones. The very first poem of *In Memoriam* presents this paralysis:

> I held it truth, with him who sings
> To one clear harp in divers tones,
> Or reach a hand thro' time to catch
> The far-off interest of tears?

The preterite "held" indicates that Tennyson can no longer share Goethe's belief in spiritual progress and survival.[22] Who can forecast the years and see whether evolution will have a suitable outcome? Who can honestly affirm that a man can evolve spiritually in this life and the next, catching the far-off interest of his tears and rising thereby to higher things? Or, even if there is material progress, if there is no survival, what comfort is it to the man living now to know that the yet-unborn will find a gain in his loss? Under such conditions, Tennyson can only give himself over to the calm despair and wild unrest that live in woe (XI, XV, XVI). His whole life becomes virtually paralyzed, with only "the sad mechanic exercise" of verse-making to numb his pain (V).

The belief that there is no human survival is portrayed by both Tennyson and Teilhard as a disabling fear that death may be stronger than love. Again, Tennyson expresses this fear at the very outset of *In Memoriam*: in the latter half of the first poem he says:

> Let Love clasp Grief lest both be drown'd,
> Let darkness keep her raven gloss.
> Ah, sweeter to be drunk with loss,
> To dance with Death, to beat the ground,
>
> Than that the victor Hours should scorn
> The long result of love, and boast,
> 'Behold the man that loved and lost,
> But all he was is overworn.'

With the passage of time, Tennyson guesses that his love for Hallam will ebb away and that the dead man will not survive even in the poet's affections. Love, Teilhard says, "becomes impoverished with remoteness in space — and still more, much more, with difference in time. For love to be possible there must be co-existence" (p. 269). But precisely because Tennyson cannot at first conceive that the dead Hallam is coexistent, he is appalled at the prospect of love's impoverishment as time draws the two men farther apart. Teilhard speaks of love as spiritual energy, but if this energy is perpetually diminished by time, man will suffer what Teilhard calls the "sickness of the dead end — the anguish of feeling shut in" (p. 228). Once more, man will sense that the "earth is darkness at the core, / And dust and ashes all that is."

The cure for this sickness lies in faith. But faith in what? Certainly not popular Christianity, with its literal reading of Genesis, its antiquated theologies, and its fierce sectarianism. That kind of Christianity cannot cure the spacetime malady because (among other reasons) it refused to see the phenomenon of man squarely. But neither Tennyson nor Teilhard rejects Christianity because some forms of it are too narrow. Instead, both men grope toward a renewed understanding of Christianity: they search for what Newman calls legitimate developments of Christian doctrine. In both Tennyson and Teilhard the shape of these developments is strikingly similar.

For one thing, both men believe in progress. So too do many other people. The important thing, however, is that Tennyson and Teilhard mean much the same thing by progress, namely spiritual growth or what Teilhard calls "hominisation" — which he defines as "the progressive phyletic spiritualisation in human civilisation of all the forces contained in the animal world" (p. 180). Too often Tennyson is regarded as the Lord Macaulay of Victorian verse, hymning the imminent brave new world of technological prosperity. But for Tennyson progress means primarily something else:

> Let knowledge grow from more to more,
>   But more of reverence in us dwell;
>   That mind and soul, according well,
> May make one music as before,
>
> But vaster.
>
> (Prologue, II. 25-29)

Tennyson does not disparage material progress, and he does want knowledge to grow from more to more. But he introduces another, more important concept of progress: the growth of reverence for some ideal manhood — in this case, the "Strong Son of God" of the Prologue. In short, Tennyson looks toward the spiritual perfection of man's humanity: "the valiant man and free, / The larger heart, the kindlier hand" (CVI.29-30).[23] Teilhard's concept of progress is similar. He too wants knowledge to grow from more to more; in fact, the increase of knowledge is one of the prerequisites of human progress (pp. 248-250). But he also believes that knowledge must contribute to increased *hominisation*. To Teilhard, progress also means increased reverence for the highest, holiest manhood. As man learns to direct his own evolution, Teilhard says, he must choose to grow into what he worships (pp. 283-285). For Teilhard, as for Tennyson, this ideal manhood is found in Christ.

Thus, both Tennyson and Teilhard believe that evolution has shifted from a biological natural selection to a spiritual growth which is partly man-controlled. In man, evolution has become conscious of itself, Teilhard says, and "for an elementary part *we hold it in our hands,* responsible for its past to its future" (p. 225). It is up to men to perfect the process of *hominisation*. This belief is precisely what Tennyson has in mind in passages like this:

> Arise and fly
>   The reeling Faun, the sensual feast;
>   Move upward, working out the beast,
> And let the ape and tiger die.[24]
>
> (CXVIII. 25-28)

To both Tennyson and Teilhard, then, progress means *hominisation*, that is, men rising on stepping stones of their dead selves to higher things.

Both agree that man's spiritual growth cannot take place in isolation. As *In Memoriam* progresses, Tennyson comes to realize that sorrowing in solitude cuts him off from the life of the world: he learns he must escape the Palace of Sorrow just as surely as the artist's soul must escape the Palace of Art. When, after much struggle, he finally declares in Poem CVIII. 1-3,

> I will not shut me from my kind,
> And, lest I stiffen into stone,
> I will not eat my heart alone.

he has made an important decision to return to life with others here on earth. For Teilhard, isolation is a blind alley to be avoided: "No evolutionary future awaits man except in association with all other men" (p. 246).[25] He condemns ideas of egocentric, racial, or national survival and exalts the concept of mega-synthesis, "the 'super-arrangement' to which *all* the thinking elements of the earth find themselves . . . subject" (p. 244; italics mine).

Both men recognize that spiritual progress will suffer setbacks and will take a long, long time. Both men feel that discouragement at the slow rate of improvement is, in Teilhard's words, "a feeling to be overcome" (p. 254). Contrary to what some critics have written, Tennyson does not believe that Utopia is just around the corner:

> No doubt vast eddies in the flood
> Of onward time shall yet be made.
>
> (CXXVIII. 5-6)

The consummation of the earth is a *far-off*, divine event.[26] Teilhard also recognizes that man has a long way to go, and he warns against feeling discouraged because of this: "After all half a million years, perhaps even a million, were required for life to pass from the pre-hominids to modern man.

Should we now start wringing our hands because, less than two centuries after glimpsing a higher state, modern man is still at loggerheads with himself?" (p. 255). For Tennyson also, discouragement is a feeling to be overcome. By refusing to shut himself from his kind, he takes a step to free himself from the anxiety that comes of realizing that "mankind is as yet on one of the lowest rungs of the ladder" (*Memoir*, I, 324). In Poem CXXVII. 1-4, he has achieved the overview that banishes discouragement:

> And all is well, tho' faith and form
> Be sunder'd in the night of fear;
> Well roars the storm to those that hear
> A deeper voice across the storm.

Both men are concerned with the problem of finding a faith for the here-and-now. Despite their attention to the goal of evolution, neither forgets that faith is valid only if it works *in the present* to nourish living men in their endeavors for the future. Once men believe that evolution can have a suitable outcome, then they can begin to work toward that outcome. With his new-found faith, Tennyson finds that he can turn from writing elegies in solitude and can move on (like the "rude swain" of Milton's *Lycidas*) to "Fresh Woods and Pastures new."[27] In Poem CVI. 19-20, Tennyson calls upon the New Year bells to "Ring out, ring out my mournful rhymes, / But ring the fuller minstrel in." Similarly, Teilhard realizes that without a particular kind of faith mankind will "go on strike," refusing the effort needed to move evolution forward (p. 305). His concern is that men should see the necessity for striving in the present, and his work is dedicated to curing the paralysis of will caused by the space-time malady. Tennyson makes the same point in Poem CXXVIII: if the changes wrought by time are merely deceptions posing as progress, then man could only scorn the whole evolutionary process. But because Tennyson can see that all is "toil cöoperant to an end" (I. 24), he can return confidently to fruitful activity.

There are, then, profound similarities between the faiths of Tennyson and Teilhard. They both believe that progress must now be spiritual, that man is at least partly responsible for the direction evolution will take, that man must grow in conjunction with all other men, that the process of *hominisation* has only begun, and that discouragement at this thought must be overcome for man to work fruitfully in the present.

We are now in a position to recognize one of the fundamental misunderstandings that led T. S. Eliot to judge the faith of *In Memoriam* as a poor thing. Tennyson, Eliot believes, tried to effect a compromise between "the religious attitude" and the Philistine belief that a materialistic Utopia was near at hand.[28] But, Eliot continues, Tennyson sensed that God and Mammon could not both be served and was not quite taken in by the very compromise he tried to effect. Eliot writes: "There is evidence elsewhere — even in an early poem, *Locksley Hall*, for example — that Tennyson by no means regarded with complacency all the changes that were going on about him in the progress of industrialism and the rise of the mercantile and manufacturing and banking classes. . . . Temperamentally, he was opposed to the doctrine that he was moved to accept and to praise."[29]

Clearly, Eliot has misjudged Tennyson's concept of progress. Tennyson never connected human perfectibility with "the progress of industrialism and the rise of the mercantile and manufacturing and banking classes." Nor did he ever believe that an imminent Utopia was taking shape in "all the changes that were going on about him." Poem CVI ("Ring out, wild bells") is almost a summary of Tennyson's idea of progress, and it is hardly a celebration of industrialism and the rise of the Philistines. Eliot has failed to distinguish between the Philistine "doctrine" of materialistic progress which Tennyson opposed and the "doctrine" of spiritual progress that he accepted and praised. This failure to distinguish between the two concepts of progress undermines Eliot's conclusion about the quality of faith in *In Memoriam*.

But to return to Tennyson and Teilhard. As persons, both men share significant characteristics. Both have a strong dash of the mystic, both have a lifelong interest in science, and both see the world from this double perspective. Both men renounce "systems" of thought. Tennyson's famous statement in the Prologue (ll. 17-18), "Our little systems have their day; / They have their day and cease to be," is paralleled by Teilhard's disclaimer in the Foreword to *The Phenomenon of Man:* "So please do not expect a final explanation of things here, nor a metaphysical system" (p. 35). Later he says, "Besides, I know the danger of trying to construct a lasting edifice with hypotheses which are only expected to last for a day, even in the minds of those who originate them" (p. 39).[30] Both men are acutely aware that knowledge grows from more to more. In both men, however, this relativity is balanced by faith in an Absolute. Both look to the future and see man evolving toward a "crowning race . . . No longer half-akin to brute" (Epilogue, ll. 128-133), or — to use Teilhard's words — toward the "hyper-personal" at Point Omega.

Both *In Memoriam* and *The Phenomenon of Man* are concerned with a faith beyond the forms of faith. Neither work seems overtly permeated by Christianity, but both are (in the authors' opinions) valid developments of it. Both men believe in a cosmic Christianity and a Christ beyond the merely sectarian Christs. Throughout *The Phenomenon of Man* Teilhard speaks primarily as a religiously neutral sage, naming the evolutionary goal as the "hyper-personal" or "Omega." Only in the Epilogue does he equate Omega with a Christ who is both the historical Jesus and the cosmic Person toward whom the whole creation moves. Tennyson sometimes speaks of the evolutionary goal in Christian terms, such as, "the Christ that is to be" (CVI. 32), but more often he too uses religiously neutral terms, such as, "the Power in darkness whom we guess" (CXXIV.4). The Prologue to *In Memoriam,* written last, is the most openly Christian part of the poem, yet it too shies away from sectarian Christianity

45

and points instead to a Christ who is both personal and cosmic. Tennyson's Prologue, however, is no more an inconsistency or an afterthought than Teilhard's Epilogue.

The Prologue to *In Memoriam* has especially puzzled many readers, but an understanding of Tennyson's cosmic Christianity helps to clarify some of its difficulties. Critics have objected to the Prologue for frequently contradictory reasons. For some, like Henry Sidgwick, "Faith, in the introduction, is too completely triumphant" (*Memoir*, I, 304). For others, it is not nearly triumphant enough, particularly in lines like: "Thou madest man, he knows not why, / He *thinks* he was not made to die" (ll. 10-11; italics mine). To some critics, the Prologue is too Christian: "There is nothing especially Christian in [*the Epilogue's*] creed of a dimly defined Deity and the progress of the universe toward some remote goal He purposes," writes Eleanor Mattes, "whereas the Prologue is in the form of a prayer to Christ, 'Strong Son of God, immortal Love,' the Word who was God's agent in the Creation."[31] To others, the Prologue is not Christian enough, especially when Tennyson apparently hesitates to affirm Christ's dual nature: "Thou *seemest* human and divine" (I. 13; italics mine). Dissatisfaction with the Prologue has caused some critics to dismiss it as an afterthought or as a muddled attempt to quiet Emily Sellwood's fears about Tennyson's religious beliefs.

But is there such confusion in the Prologue? And is there really such a discrepancy between its Christianity and the faith expressed in the rest of the poem? Not if we recognize that Tennyson is praying to a cosmic Christ — and not to the sectarian Christs preached by the churches of his day. Tennyson's Christ-that-is-to-be is a Christ to be found "when Christianity without bigotry will triumph, when the controversies of creeds shall have vanished" (*Memoir*, I, 326). Tennyson's Christ is larger than the "little systems" of nineteenth-century sectarianism can picture.

The paradox remains, however: even while affirming Christ's dual nature in the Prologue (Christ is both the

"Strong Son of God" and "the highest, holiest manhood"), Tennyson avoids a clear-cut assertion of the doctrine by saying that Christ *seems* human and divine. The contradiction is partly resolved when we see that Tennyson's hesitancy reflects his abhorrence of theological squabbling, especially about the Incarnation. "He disliked discussion on the Nature of Christ," Tennyson's son reports, " 'seeing that such discussion was mostly unprofitable, for none knoweth the Son but the Father' " (*Memoir*, I, 326). Furthermore, Tennyson was aware, as Newman was, that Christian doctrine would develop through the centuries. He knew that men might come to understand the Incarnation differently than most nineteenth-century Christians did. For Tennyson, "the forms of Christian religion would alter; but . . . the spirit of Christ would still grow from more to more 'in the roll of the ages' " (*Memoir*, I, 326).[32] The Prologue is the prayer of a man who poises belief with an awareness that his form of belief is not the last word on the subject.[33]

To say this, however, is not to say that Tennyson is hopelessly muddled in his belief. T. S. Eliot, who holds this view, writes that Tennyson "was desperately anxious to hold the faith of the believer, without being very clear about what he wanted to believe: he was capable of illumination which he was incapable of understanding. The 'Strong Son of God, immortal love', with an invocation of whom the poem opens, has only a hazy connexion with the Logos, or the Incarnate God."[34] Examined closely, Eliot's complaint is basically that Tennyson's belief is not defined in familiar, first-century terms and is therefore vague. But Tennyson was aware that first-century definitions of faith were sometimes derived from outmoded concepts of the world and needed to be re-expressed in modern terms for modern man. Teilhard explains the situation in this way:

During the first century of the Church, Christianity made its decisive entry into human thought, boldly assimilating the Jesus of the Gospels to the Logos of Alexandria. We cannot fail to see the logical sequel to this gesture and the prelude to a similar success in the

47

instinct which is today impelling the faithful, two thousand years later, to adopt the same tactics — not, this time, with the ordering principle of the static Greek kosmos, but with the neo-Logos of modern philosophy — the evolutionary principle of a universe in movement.[35]

Tennyson in *In Memoriam* is following that instinct to assimilate the historical Jesus with the neo-Logos of an evolving universe. The "hazy connexion" between the Christ of Tennyson's Prologue and the first-century Logos is Eliot's misunderstanding of the direction in which Tennyson's belief is tending: like Teilhard, Tennyson is trying to transpose belief out of "a field of thought that most modern people have left behind them."[36]

The Prologue, and indeed the whole of *In Memoriam,* indicates that Tennyson could have assented more readily to Teilhard's cosmic Christ than to the Christs preached by nineteenth-century clergymen unaware of or hostile to the world-view opened up by science. In Tennyson's day, little attention was devoted to the cosmic aspects of Pauline and Johannine teaching, and few — if any — theologians attempted to synthesize this cosmic Christianity with the recent scientific discoveries.[37] The result was, of course, that the nineteenth century produced no Aquinas to whom Tennyson could play Dante. *In Memoriam* was intended to be "a kind of *Divine Commedia*" (*Memoir,* I, 304), but Tennyson was well aware that no Angelic Doctor had appeared to reconcile "faith and form . . . sunder'd in the night of fear" (CXXVII. 1-2).

Ultimately, Tennyson and Teilhard see the universe in a process of *Christogenesis,* that is, an attempt to give birth to Christ again by evolving *AfterChrists* — to borrow Hopkins' word. There is little doubt that the three Christmases which serve as crucial landmarks in *In Memoriam* form a leitmotif emphasizing the new birth of Christ with which the universe is in labor. Like St. Paul in Romans viii. 18-27, Tennyson and Teilhard see Nature suffering birth pangs, trying to give birth to a Christ-that-is-to-be, a "Jesus, the centre towards

48

whom all moves."[38]

Both Tennyson and Teilhard see love as the spiritual energy that moves creation toward its new birth. Teilhard argues that love has a long evolutionary history: "If there were no internal propensity to unite, even at a prodigiously rudimentary level — indeed in the molecule itself — it would be physically impossible for love to appear higher up, with us, in 'hominised' form" (p. 264). Teilhard sees love as the sign of successful "involution" in the universe: love is "the more or less direct trace marked on the heart of the element by the psychical convergence of the universe upon itself" (p. 265). Thus, human love — in all its varied forms — is the highest evolutionary manifestation of the energy that drives creation toward universal convergence and is itself the sign of that movement.

Again, what the scientist speaks of in general terms, the poet portrays in personal ones. When Tennyson speaks of love, he usually means his own love for Hallam: this is the love that he fears in Poem I will be drowned unless it clings to grief. But as Tennyson becomes increasingly aware in *In Memoriam* that the dead Hallam is (to use Teilhard's term) "co-existent" with himself, he discovers that love is stronger than death. His love has not been impoverished by remoteness in space or difference in time, as the experience of Poem XCV demonstrates. With this awareness, Tennyson can again believe in a cosmic love that can bring about a suitable outcome to evolution:

> The love that rose on stronger wings,
>   Unpalsied when he met with Death,
>   Is comrade of the lesser faith
> That sees the course of human things.
>
> (CXVIII. 1-4)

Tennyson has come to recognize that his own love for Hallam is a particular, direct trace of the universal psychical convergence. If his love for Hallam can survive death and can grow into "vaster passion," then there is hope that the larger, cosmic pattern of convergence can be fulfilled: "Behold, I dream a dream of good, / And mingle all the world with thee" (CXXIX. 11-12).

It is no "semantic sleight-of-hand" when Tennyson, in the Prologue, identifies "immortal Love" with Christ.[39] Just as Dante sees in his love for Beatrice a reflection of and a participation in the Love that moves the sun and other stars, so also Tennyson comes to see in his love for Hallam a reflection of and a participation in the immortal Love toward whom the whole creation moves. For Tennyson, love is ultimately a Person — Christ in the Prologue, God in the Epilogue. And here again he agrees with Teilhard. For Teilhard, Omega is in the final analysis a "supremely attractive" Person, whom he names God-Omega (p. 287) and Christ (p. 297).

The identification of Love with Christ in the Prologue of *In Memoriam* should awaken us to hints that appear in the body of the poem: if we read carefully, we can see Tennyson working toward this identification within the poem. (The process resembles that in Newman's *Apologia:* at the outset, we know that Newman is going to identify truth with Roman Catholic doctrine, and as we read, we watch him working toward that identification.) Throughout *In Memoriam* itself, Tennyson focuses on Hallam, but the figure of Christ is always present in the background.[40] Hallam, Tennyson comes to recognize, is "a noble type" of the ideal man, an *AfterChrist* or *BeforeOmega,* who awakens Tennyson to "the highest, holiest manhood" found in Christ. It is fitting, therefore, that Hallam's birthday be celebrated as another Christmas, as it indeed is in Poem CVII. As *AfterChrist,* Hallam shares the human-divine nature (CXXIX.5); as *BeforeOmega,* he reconciles God and Nature, thereby indicating in his own self that evolution can have both a suitable outcome and a focus (CXXX). The dead Hallam thus shows forth the divine love to Tennyson just as the dead Beatrice did to Dante. Like the just man in Hopkins' sonnet, Hallam "acts in God's eye what in God's

50

eye he is — /Christ."[41] Teilhard explains the process this way: in order for man to love Omega, this supremely attractive Prime Mover Ahead must somehow be present to man now. Space and time impoverish love, Teilhard says; therefore, "to be supremely attractive, Omega must be supremely present" (p. 269). In *In Memoriam* Tennyson discovers that Christ-Omega is supremely present in Hallam. Thus, to both Tennyson and Teilhard, the focus of evolution is at times in sight even now, and this vision of the end, present even now, enables men to continue striving toward the one far-off divine event at Point Omega.

In addition to the similarity of vision shared by Tennyson and Teilhard, there is also a similarity of technique. Neither man attempts merely to argue the reader into assent. Both are aware, with Newman, that "the whole man" is involved in Real Assent. Rational or logical arguments can win Notional Assent, that is, agreement to intellectual propositions. To win Real Assent, the whole man must be engaged and must share the same vision as the writer. This is what both Tennyson and Teilhard attempt to do. *In Memoriam* has its "structure" of sorts, *The Phenomenon of Man* has its "rational" framework, but both works recreate experiences which the reader shares. By living through the same experiences as the writer, the reader is slowly led to accept the same conclusions that the writer was forced to accept. There is nothing deceptive about this persuasive technique: the writer uses art to revivify the experience which led him to his faith; the reader, by reading the work, is put through a similar experience and is led to assent (if he can) to the writer's beliefs.

Teilhard is not just a philosopher whose thought can be epitomized. Rather, he is a sage with a vision to communicate. In the Foreword to *The Phenomenon of Man* he says that his work "may be summed up as an attempt *to see* and *to show* what happens to man, and what conclusions are forced upon us, when he is placed fairly and squarely within the framework of phenomenon and appearance" (p. 31).

51

Like the Victorian sages discussed by John Holloway, Teilhard's "main task is to quicken his reader's perceptiveness; and he does this by making a far wider appeal than the exclusively rational appeal. . . . He gives expression to his outlook imaginatively."[42] In Teilhard's book, the reader is given an overview of the phenomenon of man, from its primitive origins in the "stuff of the universe," to its present spiritual crisis, to its future evolution. This survey, however, is more than just a scientific treatise; it is an artistically constructed narrative told by a skillfully created persona. When, for example, Teilhard concludes a section of his book with the solemn words, "Thought is born" (p. 160), this brief dramatic sentence is a carefully prepared-for climax, designed to awaken in the reader a sense of the awesomeness of what has happened. Images are used to clarify and actualize abstract concepts; some images, like "the great spiral of life," form leitmotifs. Words are used connotatively as well as denotatively. For example, discussing the "noosphere," the envelope of thought and culture that man lives in, Teilhard concludes:

> With that [awareness of the noosphere] it bursts upon us how utterly warped is every classification of the living world . . . in which man only figures logically as a *genus* or a new family. This is an error of perspective which deforms and uncrowns the whole phenomenon of the universe. To give man his true place in nature it is not enough to find one more pigeon-hole in the edifice of our systemisation or even an additional order or branch. With hominisation, in spite of the insignificance of the anatomical leap, we have the beginning of a new age. The earth 'gets a new skin.' Better still, it finds its soul. (p. 182)

Even in translation, the passage bristles with emotion evoked to a great extent by skillful word choices. This is hardly the place for an extended study of the art of *The Phenomenon of Man*, but any account of the book must recognize that art is a fundamental part of its effort to win the reader's assent.

Similarly, Tennyson uses art to reconstruct his own experiences after Hallam's death. With Tennyson — or, more accurately, with the speaker in the poem — the reader relives the shock of loss, the collapse of faith, the struggle to achieve emotional balance, the slowly dawning awareness of hope and faith, the mystical intuitions, and the final release of returning joy. Tennyson also uses art to show man placed squarely within the framework of phenomenon and appearance. Like Teilhard, he attempts to make us *see* the work of time. When the poem has been experienced, the reader can understand at least how the speaker has achieved his final faith. But perhaps the reader will also recognize the inherent rightness of that faith. If the poet's vision is valid, if his art is skillful, and if the reader's mind and heart are right, then there is a good chance that poet and reader will be in accord when the poem reaches its conclusion.

In any event, it is time to re-evaluate the quality of faith in *In Memoriam*. If Teilhard's "work gives our generation the comprehensive view it sorely needs," as Arnold J. Toynbee says, then the faith of *In Memoriam* — with its many resemblances to Teilhard's vision — cannot be dismissed as a poor thing.

NOTES

1. T. S. Eliot, "In Memoriam," *Essays Ancient and Modern* (London: Faber, 1936), p. 187.

2. Kenneth Allott (ed.), *The Poems of Matthew Arnold* (New York: Barnes & Noble, 1965), p. 341. See Allott's note to ll. 182-190 identifying Tennyson as the poet referred to in these lines.

3. Harold Nicolson, *Tennyson: Aspects of His Life, Character, and Poetry*, rev. ed. (Garden City, N.Y.: Doubleday, 1962), p. 299. This book was originally published in 1923.

4. Some notable exceptions: Basil Willey, "Tennyson," *More Nineteenth Century Studies: A Group of Honest Doubters* (New York: Columbia University Press, 1966); Jerome Hamilton Buckley, *Tennyson: The Growth of a Poet* (Boston: Houghton Mifflin Company, 1965); and Carlisle Moore, "Faith, Doubt, and Mystical Experience in *In Memoriam.*" VS. 7 (1963): 155-169.

5. E. D. H. Johnson, *The Alien Vision of Victorian Poetry* (Hamden, Conn.: The Shoe String Press, 1963), p. 21.

6. "The Poetry of Tennyson," *From Dickens to Hardy,* ed. Boris Ford (Harmondsworth, Middlesex, 1958), pp. 243-244, n. 13.

7. Valerie Pitt, *Tennyson Laureate* (Toronto: U. of Toronto Press, 1963), p. 101.

8. George O. Marshall, *Tennyson Handbook* (New York, 1963), p. 122.

9. Quoted in Hallam Lord Tennyson, *Alfred Lord Tennyson: A Memoir*, I (New York, 1897), 304-305 — hereafter cited as *Memoir*.

10. See especially Dorothy L. Sayers' introductions and notes to *The Comedy of Dante Alighieri the Florentine*, trans. Dorothy L. Sayers and Barbara Reynolds, 3 vols. (Baltimore: Penguin Books, 1949-62); and C. S. Lewis, Preface to *Paradise Lost* (New York: Oxford University Press, 1961).

11. There is no question of "influence" here: Tennyson did not influence Teilhard any more than he influenced Darwin. On Tennyson's anticipating Darwin, see Willey, "Tennyson," *More Studies*, p. 87, and Buckley, *Tennyson*, p. 121.

12. Pierre Teilhard de Chardin, *The Phenomenon of Man*, tr. Bernard Wall (New York: Harper & Row, 1961), p. 31. Unless otherwise noted, all references to Teilhard's writing are to this text.

   I am grateful to Eulalio R. Baltazar and Peter J. Fellenz of the University of Dayton Department of Theology for reading an early draft of this paper. Any errors in the final version of the paper are, of course, the responsibility of the author. Baltazar's *Teilhard and the Supernatural* (Baltimore: Helicon, 1966), although not quoted in this paper, is an extremely useful study of Teilhard's thought.

13. *In Memoriam* CXVIII. 7-12. All quotations from Tennyson's poetry are taken from *Works*, ed. Hallam Lord Tennyson, 6 vols. (New York: Macmillan Company, 1908).

14. Buckley, *Tennyson*, p. 276, n. 16.

15. Willey, "Tennyson," *More Studies*, pp. 83-84.

16. A. C. Bradley, *A Miscellany* (London: Macmillan Company, 1929), p. 31.

17. Throughout the paper Tennyson is referred to as the speaker in the poem. An absolute identification of author and speaker is questionable, however, because the poem is not strictly autobiographical. See *Memoir*, I, 304.

18. Mayhead, "Tennyson," *From Dickens to Hardy*, p. 239.

19. See, e.g., ll. 22-30.

20. Quoted in Claude Cuénot, *Teilhard de Chardin*, tr. Vincent Colimore (Baltimore: Helicon, 1965), p. 158.

21. Quoted in Cuénot, p. 158.

22. For the identification of "him who sings," see *Memoir*, II, 391 and n. With the reading of Poem I given here, cf. Lore Metzger, "The Eternal Process: Some Parallels Between Goethe's *Faust* and Tennyson's *In Memoriam*," *Victorian Poetry*, I (1963): 189-196.

23. Cf. *Locksley Hall Sixty Years After*, I. 276: "Forward, till you see the highest Human Nature is divine."

24. Valerie Pitt objects to this passage: "The modern mind can scarce endure this; moral endeavor is not its ideal, and it recognises that the energies of the ape and tiger are not without their place in the higher life of man" (*Tennyson Laureate*, pp. 113-114). It is difficult to quarrel with generalizations about "the modern mind," but Basil Willey apparently disagrees with Miss Pitt about it: "We have rightly learned from the nineteenth century that man must make himself, and be the changer as well as the product of his own environment. But we must also learn that if man makes himself wholly in his own image, he may find that like Frankenstein he has created his own destroyer" ("Origins and Development of the Idea of Progress," *Ideas and Beliefs of the Victorians* [New York: E. P. Dutton & Co., 1966], p. 39). Also, has Miss Pitt confused Tennyson's tiger with Blake's? To Tennyson, the ape and tiger in *In Memoriam* represent only unreflecting animalism. Is it accurate to see in them energies that have their place in the higher life of man? Do they not function much as Dante's leopard, lion, and shewolf do in Canto i of Hell, that is, as symbols of what obstructs man in his efforts to climb higher?

   With Tennyson's idea, cf. Teilhard's statement: "See how the animals behave (monkeys, for example, or even certain insects): we see them doing things that are materially culpable, and only need the emergence of a fuller consciousness to become fully reprehensible." Quoted in Henri de Lubac, *Teilhard de Chardin: The Man and His Meaning*, tr. René Hague (New York: New American Library, 1967), p. 101, n. 16.

25. Cf. a canceled section of *In Memoriam* (originally CXXVII) in which Tennyson calls upon the "Victor Hours" to "fuse the peoples into one" (*Memoir*, I, 307).

26. *The Idylls of the King*, describing the deterioration of King Arthur's civilization, is devoted primarily to depicting one such eddy in the flood. In *Locksley Hall Sixty Years After*, the old man says (ll. 235-236):

   > Foreward then, but still remember how the course of Time
   > will serve,
   > Crook and turn upon itself in many a backward streaming
   > curve.

27. Cf. Joseph Sendry, "*In Memoriam* and *Lycidas*," PMLA, 82 (October 1967): 437-443.

28. "In Memoriam," *Essays*, p. 187.

29. "In Memoriam," *Essays*, p. 187.

30. Cf. de Lubac, *Teilhard*, p. 97: "Moreover, [Teilhard] never

achieved a definite formulation of his thought, nor did he ever claim to provide a complete theological or dogmatic exposition."

31. Eleanor Mattes, *In Memoriam: The Way of a Soul* (New York: Exposition, 1951), p. 91. It is interesting to note that while Mrs. Mattes immediately identifies the "Strong Son of God" with the Word of God, or the Logos, T. S. Eliot finds only a "hazy connexion" between the two. See below in text.

32. Cf. Teilhard's "O Christ, ever greater!" See de Lubac, *Teilhard*, pp. 45-54.

33. Cf. Memoir, I, 309-312, where Tennyson's "reverent impatience of formal dogma" is discussed. Note that Tennyson's attitude is different from poising belief with unbelief, as exemplified in the famous prayer: "O God, if there is a God, save my soul, if I have a soul."

34. Eliot, "In Memoriam," *Essays*, pp. 184-185.

35. Quoted in de Lubac, *Teilhard*, p. 38.

36. Teilhard de Chardin, quoted in de Lubac, *Teilhard*, p. 116.

37. See de Lubac, *Teilhard*, p. 44.

38. Quoted in de Lubac, *Teilhard*, p. 44.

39. See Pitt, *Tennyson Laureate*, p. 115.

40. See, E.G., the three Christmasses in XXVIII, XXIX, XXX, LXXVIII, CIV, and CV; as well as XXXI, XXXII, XXXVI, LXIX, and CVI.

41. W. H. Gardner and N. H. MacKenzie, eds., *Poems of Gerard Manley Hopkins*, 4th ed. (London: Oxford University Press, 1967), p. 90.

42. John Holloway, *The Victorian Sage* (New York: W. W. Norton & Company, 1965), p. 10.

TEILHARD, NEO-MARXISM, EXISTENTIALISM: A CONFRONTATION
Madeleine Barthelemy-Madaule

We must begin by justifying our project. Is a genuine encounter possible between the thought of Teilhard de Chardin and any purely philosophical system? The fact that they ask the same questions, that they propose analogous answers, that they open up similar horizons of thought — this is not yet enough to make a dialogue possible. The true meeting ground must be on the meaning of man. But this is a religious as well as a philosophical question. And if the thought of Teilhard were exclusively religious, on what common ground could it meet with a philosophy? Even if it were religious only in its basic postulates and from then on were to take on the trappings of a philosophical system, there could still be no basis for a genuine encounter. Hence our first task must be to distinguish the philosophical attitude from the religious — without embarking, however, on a detailed comparative analysis of philosophy and religion.

The characteristic note of the religious attitude is docile attentiveness to what is understood as the Transcendent and received as such without question. It makes no initial appeal to rational criticism; neither does it reject it. What it requires first and foremost is the adherence of the whole mind and the whole will. It calls for a decision, a commitment, an act of trust; then, supported by these, a freely willed self-sub-

From *International Philosophical Quarterly*, 1 (December, 1961): 648-667. Reprinted by permission of the publisher.

mission. This religious attitude can exist even outside the context of all transcendent religion; but in this case it becomes a monstrous aberration.

The philosophical attitude is quite the reverse. In contrast to this abdication of the critical spirit, whether legitimate or not, it is essentially a free exercise of the human mind. I am not here identifying all philosophy with rationalism. It is a question rather of a basic attitude that precedes all particular philosophical positions. If one wishes to be a philosopher, there is no help for it but to enter upon the path of critical reflection, at least to some minimum degree. The problematic of Socrates, the doubt of Descartes, etc. — all point to the philosopher's determination to think things through, even at the expense, if need be, of his most cherished inclinations. The idealism of Kant represents, perhaps at its highest intensity, this uncompromising loyalty of the mind to its own exigencies, carried all the way to heroism. The anguish of Kierkegaard is a manifestation of the same attitude less remote from Kant than is commonly believed.

How then could we philosophers find any common ground with someone like Teilhard de Chardin if the core of his thought were an experience of the divine to be communicated only by a kind of spiritual contagion? In that case his proper place would be rather in the ranks of the saints, whose very existence is a summons to us. If he had not placed himself on the level of a universally communicable intellectual experience, we could indeed become his faithful devotees. But we would have no right to call ourselves his *intellectual* disciples.

Yet the fact of the matter is that the intention of Teilhard's thought was to reach every intelligence as such, and for that very reason expressed itself in the language of reason. "Everything must pass through the crucible of thought," he reminds us at the beginning of *Comment je vois*.

Still, it may be objected, even though his language may be universal, it is not for all that philosophical. Spirituality or science, perhaps, but not philosophy. And yet a good number of his smaller works, not to mention *The Phenomenon of Man,* undeniably contain an all-embracing vision of man and the universe. Whether or not one is willing to call this a "philosophy," at least one cannot deny that there is a philosophical dimension to it. Philosophers must resign themselves, whether they like it or not, to come to grips with this thinker, even if the various labels with which they attempt to classify him shatter against the hard crystal of his thought. Spiritualism, materialism, etc. — all are so many roadmarkers which point the way to an intuition that has no need of them in order to express itself, since it is rather they that are illumined by it.

Commentators have always taken more pains to classify creative thinkers than the latter have themselves. Opposing sides are still claiming Descartes as their own. If Kant can be categorized, it is he himself who has supplied the terms in which to do so. Before him, who ever heard of "transcendental idealism"? If the vision of Teilhard is indeed new, we must resign ourselves to scrap existing categories when dealing with him, or even to forge new ones. From now on, therefore, let us speak in terms not of "system" (though he himself sometimes uses the term to signify coherence of thought) but of "open perspective." To be more exact, he prefers to speak of a "sheaf of axes," deep within reality, "along which progress can flow." These are open roads, so to speak, with no terminus yet in sight, somewhat like Bergson's "lines of probability."

In sum, a confrontation is possible, nay unavoidable, between Teilhard and contemporary philosophers. Even if he himself never engaged precisely in the work of a philosopher, he has at least written the introduction and the prolegomena to a future philosophical vision of the world. Let us therefore consider this preliminary question settled and the way cleared for the execution of our project.

We have chosen to confront the thought of Pierre Teilhard de Chardin first with Neo-Marxism, then with existentialism. There are good reasons for this choice. First, if one examines his writings without preconceived ideas, one cannot but be struck by the key role accorded therein to the human anxiety and anguish characteristic of our times, as well as to the determination to transcend them without taking refuge in illusory solutions. It is precisely because existentialism assumes this anguish as its own and because Marxism lays claim to have found the solution to it that both of these philosophical positions are the kind that would naturally interest Teilhard. A question which deliberately wills to remain without an answer (existentialism) and an answer which does not fulfill the expectations of the question (Marxism) — such are the two extremes between which the dialectic of his thought unfolds. The added fact that these two poles have become the most sensitive and crucial points of controversy for the contemporary mind is our second reason for choosing them as points of comparison with the thought of Teilhard.

We might add that in carrying out such a confrontation we may well be approaching closer than at first appears to an eventual dialogue of the dead between Immanuel Kant and Pierre Teilhard de Chardin. For behind the existential anguish which results from the barring of all access to the Absolute by the forces of reason, no less than behind the humanistic rationalism which deliberately excludes all metaphysics as a blind alley, walks the shadow of the philosopher of Koenigsberg, author of the boast, "I have destroyed all metaphysics."

Such is the *raison d'etre* of this article. As we begin, the first point to note is that the attitude of Teilhard implies both a method and a metaphysics. Both flow from his initial assumption of an angle of vision on the universe. This consists in contemplating the world from such a height that he is able to discern at once the present fragmentation of contemporary humanity in its pursuit of multiplicity and the point of unity ahead, illumined by hope, towards which it is striving. Looked at from this perspective, each of the great directions of thought we are dealing with contain a measure of truth that the other leaves in the shadow. But each is also in the last analysis an error, to the extent that, incomplete though it be, it looks on itself with complacency as the whole truth. At this moment it becomes imprisoned in its own chains and takes on the wild look either of radical despair or of fanatical certitude. To liberate these fragments of truth and point the way to their future synthesis lies in the power of only a few lonely seers who stand out like lighthouses probing into the mists of the future. Yet each one of us is capable in some measure of reflecting their light; for there is no one truly a man in our day who, despite his resistance to these currents of thought, does not feel strong within him the alternate pull now of anxiety, now of the new faith in man.

"Whether one shares in its worship or ridicules it, who in our day can escape being haunted, even obsessed, by the idea of Humanity?"[1] No reader of Teilhard can fail to remember the page on which these words appear. But not nearly so many are familiar with the remarkable lines in which, picturing the Christian in the world of the laboratory, he speaks of two faiths confronting each other: faith in God and faith in the world. His assertion that "everyone engaged in research is committed to faith in the forward march of progress"[2] is well illustrated by the verses of the poet Louis Aragon on Joliot-Curie, the scientist:

> ...... dans les temps ou nous sommes
> Nous comprenons tout autrement la grandeur, la beaute morale,
> Et ce que cherche Joliot c'est le bonheur de tous les hommes.
> Il n'y a plus de chevaliers que pour la quete de ce Graal.

This new religion, if we may so call it, has been developing now for several centuries. The scientific flowering of the sixteenth century, the spirit of independent religious criticism developed by the Reformation, the spirit of independent philosophical criticism stemming from Cartesianism, the whole critical enterprise of the Encyclopedists, Kant's indictment of metaphysics, the realization of the loneliness of a world without God in the nineteenth century ("God is dead") — these are the main stages along a road which was to end up, on the one hand, with the "Credo quia absurdum" of Kierkegaard and Chestov or the "absurdum sine credo" of Heidegger and Sartre, and on the other, with the powerful anti-metaphysical rationalism of Karl Marx.

Not that there is any strict necessity in the line followed by this development. Another terminal point would have commanded another curve of evolution, with different stages along the way. But it is the present course of events which has actually worked itself out in history. And what is peculiarly significant is that the Marxism in which it culminates has not been content merely to give expression to the world it has found. It has radically transformed it. For even if the new humanism reigns only in the East, it is now firmly planted also like a thorn in the flesh of the world we call "the west."

Father Teilhard laid his finger with precision on the true foundation stone of dialectical materialism. It is the rejection of all transcendence and the conviction that the destiny and meaning of man are played out on this earth alone. Accordingly, he suggests the term *Terrenisme* to designate Communism. Humanity and science are the objects of its faith, its absolute. Marx and Engels, it is true, sounded the death-knell of all eternal truths (especially in the Anti-Duhring). But did they foresee in their disciples or recognize within themselves the premonitions of a coming shift in the very meaning of the absolute? Be this as it may, it remains true that earthly man is profoundly rooted in the matter from which he has little by little emerged. Once having succeeded in painfully disengaging his individuality, he is now on the road to a stage of truly planetary collectivization. How can we fail to admit the essential truth of all this? The role of matter, the history of the world and of man within it, the primary place of science, the movement towards collectivism — all these are incontestable facts. Why is it that Karl Marx's synthesis of all these truths is not itself a truth?

To reply to this question requires a patient penetration into what the author of *The Phenomenon of Man* meditated on more and more deeply as he advanced in years.[3] His meditations and reflections focus on two different levels according as they are concerned with the element of religious aspiration contained in Marxism — which leads him to compare it with Christianity — or with its political aspect — which leads him to compare it with its rival political currents, fascism or democracy. (These parallels, of course, imply no equivalence of the terms of comparison, only a coexistence in fact.)

Let us begin with the political level and ascend from it to the religious. The three dominant preoccupations of the man of today are with the future, the universal, and the personal. These notions were, of course, known and respected by the classical thinkers. But before the present century they were never tangible realities. The future came in prominence when the action of time began to gain a central place, during the eighteenth and nineteenth centuries, in biology, in sociology, and finally even in physics. Historical process invaded all fields, and along with it progress and the dominance of the future. The universal became a truly vital concept when the planetary repercussions of all phenomena came to be recognized. Finally, the dimension of the personal emerged with the recognition of the rights of the individual. What had formerly been merely conceptual now became a lived awareness.

Now what actually happened is that each great political current sponsored, so to speak, one of these goals and neglected the others. And the presence of this one goal in each case became more and more distorted by the absence of the others, which by right form together with it one single and indivisible truth. Thus communism without a doubt has its eyes fixed on the future and on the universal through the medium of socialization and global planning. It is quite correct in rooting the work of man in the depths of "the matrix of matter." But in its determination to struggle against the excesses of liberty and individualism characteristic of the democracy of 1789, it ends up by menacing the legitimate freedom of the person. Bent upon imposing socialization at all costs, it ends up by seriously threatening not only the individual person but also the very collectivity it is aiming at, which cannot be obtained by coercion but must ripen from within by the power of persuasion. Finally, in reacting against a disincarnated spiritualism it ends up by going too far and losing the spiritual entirely. All the above deficiencies have as both their source and their term a vision that is too shortsighted:

> If man does not recognize the authentic nature and the authentic object of his love, the result is profound and irremediable disorder. Fiercely determined to satisfy with too restricted an object a longing all-embracing in its scope, he will inevitably attempt to compensate for this fundamental unbalance by the materiality and ever increasing multiplicity of his experiences.[4]

What the vision of Teilhard is attempting to do, therefore, is to incorporate into a Christian synthesis the exigencies of Marxism that express the legitimate needs of modern man. Social unification, the progress of technology, and the advance of thought are the fundations of man's power and of his confidence in himself. But because human beings are centers of reflection, they cannot truly unite with each other save by intensifying their activity as conscious centers, that is to say, their personalities. As Teilhard has put it:

> It seems clear enough that the latest experiments of totalitarianism allow us to pass a decisive judgment on this point. If the "particles" of a social group are linked together externally by coercion, their only bond being their function in society, they inevitably deteriorate and regress; they become mechanized.[5]

Only a union from within, center to center, "possesses the property not only of differentiating but of personalizing the elements that it organizes."[6] This union is a work of slow maturation. The mutual attraction between men, which is its necessary condition of possibility, is bound up with the

> ... radiation from some ultimate center (at once transcendent and immanent) of psychic unification, the same, in fact, whose existence, by opening up to human action an outlet into the irreversible future, reveals itself as indispensable (the crucial requirement for anything in the future) in order to preserve the zest for progress despite the surrounding shadows of death.[7]

If we examine Teilhard's criticisms of Marxism in the light of his overall vision, their positive aspect will emerge. In daring to reach out all the way to the ultimate center, he has no intention of engaging in Utopian thinking of the type that would lose sight of the present in its concentration on ultimate horizons. His aim is rather to give to human effort the only meaning that renders it coherent at all. The divine center is, in fact, the only point of equilibrium (from above) which is capable of allowing an ever fuller self-affirmation to individual liberties in proportion as their social integration becomes more intense and more irreversible. It is the final goal that guarantees the ascending drive towards a spirit more and more disengaged from matter, yet with its original rooting in matter still intact.

This process of the transmutation of matter into spirit is the cosmic aspect of what Father Teilhard called "the Christic" and which dominated his latest thinking. By transcending death the God of Christianity is alone capable of saving the work of humanity. Could our feeling for the Absolute ever be satisfied merely by the progress of humanity, by a more just and fraternal human city, if their only support were in perishable this-worldly roots?

> But will not the work itself of our minds, of our hearts and of our hands — that is to say, our achievements, our products, our *opus* — will not this, too, in some sense be "eternalised" and saved? Indeed, Lord, it will be — in virtue of a need that You Yourself have implanted at the very center of my will. I desire and need that it should be.[8]

Our works? But even in the interest of life in general, what is the work of human works if not to establish, in and by means of each one of us, an absolutely original centre in which the universe reflects itself in a unique and inimitable way? And those centres are our very selves and personalities.[9]

It is fascinating to see how Teilhard on the one hand exalts the invisible effort of personalization in *The Phenomenon of Man* and on the other the elevation of transfigured human achievements in *The Divine Milieu.* The completely synthetic character of his thought shines forth here at its clearest. He gives due credit to the demand for earthly effectiveness while at the same time reminding us that this is of itself worthless unless dominated by persons. He penetrates more deeply into the elevation of the person precisely by presenting it in all its wholeness, that is, with the harvest of its external works joined inseparably to its interior intentions.

Thus we can affirm without fear of contradiction that to the human realities highlighted by Marxism correspond always the essential points of Teilhard's own vision. On each major theme we could quote parallel passages — parallel, not equivalent.

"And therefore even on the plane of devotion to the world I can say legitimately and with pride to my humanist or Marxist comrade: *plus ego.*" This sentence from an unpublished work was expanded magnificently in *The Divine Milieu:* "How could we be deserters, or sceptical about the future of the tangible world? . . . How little you know us!" Thus it is really to a wider vision that Teilhard invites the Marxist masses to open their eyes: "It is here that you are not yet human enough, you do not go *to the limits* of your humanity."[10]

Thus humanism is invited to expand to its full metaphysical dimensions. The stake involved is the fulfillment of the life of the spirit. We have been stifling under too low a sky of purely human doctrines. But — this, too, needs to be said — we have also lost our bearings under the too distant sky of a distorted and disincarnated Christianity. The "Christic" experience that is without doubt the most profound and most personal contribution of Teilhard is in the line of the "above" and the "up ahead" (*l'en haut et l'en avant*). It alone can baptize, i.e., give new birth in the waters of baptism to, the effort of the communists.

There is nothing here resembling a facile concordism, but rather the authentic witness of a man who, out of the total honesty of his reflection, affirmed that he would without a doubt have been led to become a Christian by the very movement of his research even if he had not been one already. Marxism is capable, Teilhard believed and hoped, of opening itself to the spiritual. The Christian on his side can open himself to the world. But on either side they are quite capable of not doing so. For it is the characteristic of man to take into his own hands the tiller of evolution and not merely to be guided by it. Does not such a perspective contain all the elements of a tragic optimism? Or rather, may we suggest the term "dramatic optimism?" By this we mean to exclude the irremediable, fatalistic dimension of tragedy, while preserving the aspect of anxiety and risk proper to a drama which necessarily involves bloody wounds and tears but not total and ultimate destruction of the essential. This dramatic optimism is defined in terms of a synthesis of humanism and Christianity.

The perspective of Teilhard is centered on a two-fold experience: of fullness and of need, of joy and of anxiety.[11] The intuitive and dialectical unfolding of this thought is a perpetual effort to transcend this duality. His earliest childhood memories are of "adoration" of the durable (the hardest metal, "my iron God") and of despair before the corruptible (a lock of hair burning up in the fire, a piece of rusting iron, etc.). Later on the most intimate texts, in the form of stories, speak allegorically of the presence of Being, followed by its withdrawal. Anxiety is thus not the sole point of reference of his interior life, but one of two; the other is faith.

Teilhard's whole construction is thought out in function

of the anxiety of our day. *The Divine Milieu, The Phenomenon of Man,* and the *Singularites de l'espece humaine* all contain important pages on this theme. But it is to *The Divine Milieu* that we must go to find the *interior experience* of this anxiety and the living witness to it: "I took the lamp and, leaving the zone of everyday occupations and relationships where everything seems clear, I went down into my inmost self, to the deep abyss whence I felt dimly that my power of action emanates." In proportion as he descends deeper, he finds himself slipping away from his own self: "And when I had to stop my exploration because the path faded from beneath my steps, I found a bottomless abyss at my feet." Faced with it, the mind "reels." It is "troubled" and vacillates back and forth. "I felt the essential distress of an atom lost in the universe, the distress which makes human wills founder daily under the crushing number of living things and of stars."[12]

The movement of thought here is very close to that of Pascal. Man wants to measure first himself and then the world. As soon as he attempts to do it he recoils in fear. For if his own most intimate depths open out into an abyss, the world on its side is equally frightening. "How precarious this habitation is! At any moment the vast and horrible thing may break in through the cracks — through every opening, the great horror pours in upon us, the thing which we try hard to forget is always there, separated from us by a flimsy partition."[13]

It is at this point that man's call to God breaks forth and God's call to man is heard in reply. Perhaps indeed they are but one and the same thing: God present within us in the very cry which invokes Him. "And if I was saved it was by hearing the voice of the Gospels which spoke to me from the depths of my night: 'It is I. Fear not.' "[14] This was the presence of God. It is an answer to man's reaching out: "In order that I may not yield to the temptation to curse the universe and the one who made it, help me to adore it by seeing you hidden within it."[15]

Few passages in existentialist philosophy sketch so powerfully the royal road from despair to God. We must go further: this anguish is itself His Presence. "Truly even sad and somber things themselves, the phantom, the storm, are, if we wish, your own self." Even the leap over the chasm between finite and infinite is here abolished. A lightning flash of synthesis takes the place of the leap. The paradox is gathered up into a single point:

> Let us only believe, let us believe the more strongly and desperately in proportion as reality appears more menacing and irreducible. And then, little by little, we shall see the universal horror relax, then smile upon us, then take us into its more than human arms.[16]

One would think that the opponents of Teilhard de Chardin had never read these texts. If they had, would they have reproached him for his optimism? All one can say to those who judge him on some preconceived idea is: "Read him, I beg you, read him." Then they could not help but hear the voice of a man on the Mount of Olives.

The meaning of this anguish is not restricted to the psychological terrain into which it sinks its roots. It is not a question merely of an episode in an individual's life. It is the state of the human condition itself. It is not a timeless concept. It is a lived existential experience of our contemporary world. Moreover, it is destined to become more intense as man realizes more fully his humanity. In its primitive form it is linked with the emergence of the reign of man, or, as Teilhard puts it, it is linked to the "inner summons to change." In a conference at the Centre de Synthese, Jankelevitch, who is not a Teilhard sympathizer, wrote that anxiety is "the very core of change itself," it is the reaction in the presence of the "not yet visible order to come." To assert that anxiety is congenital to man is to say that it is inseparable from reflection and liberty: "It is man with the freedom to give himself to effort or draw back from it, man with the frightening power to criticize life and take its measure."[17]

Anxiety is so closely bound up with liberty and thought

that the world (i.e., the human world) could, on coming face to face with itself by reflection, refuse to accept itself. But liberty in Teilhard's perspective involves much more than merely subjective possibilities. It implicates a whole universe in which it in turn is implicated. Its anxiety arises in the face of an eventual "radical absurdity of the universe."[18]

This is truly existential anxiety, and its "unmotivated" character, together with the haziness and diffuseness of its metaphsical vision, that is, its absence of determinate object, did not escape Teilhard's notice. That is why he distinguished it from simple fear. Its effect could well be the revolt we spoke of above, this saying "No" to being, or this "disgust with living" that he dreaded most of all — so much so that he devoted an important smaller work to "the taste for life."

All this is the risk of freedom. And we can meet the challenge only by clearly facing the dilemma, by making an option,[19] or even a wager:

> Either nature is closed to our demands for futurity, in which case thought, the fruit of millions of years of effort, is stifled, still-born in a self-abortive and absurd universe. Or else an opening exists . . . ; but in that case the way out, if we are to agree to embark upon it, must open out freely onto limitless psychic spaces in a universe to which we can unhesitatingly entrust ourselves.[20]

Yet this is not the wager of Pascal; for the scale is weighted on the side of one of the alternatives by logic and in some way by the promises of a whole world. It is precisely here that Teilhard's dramatic optimism fits in, which is indeed existential, but not existentialist. The fears of the human race are not identical with the radical anxiety we have spoken of, and yet they are linked to it; for each particular fear opens up, at the precise point that gives occasion to it, a breach through which pours in the "ontological infinity" of anxiety. It is thus, for example, that on the occasion of some tiny disappointment there sometimes pours in upon us an ocean of misery out of all proportion to the incident that caused it.

The fears of the human race increase with the growing menace of collectivism for the individual. The latter stands at the threshold of mass absorption into humanity as a group, as a result of the proliferation of its numbers and the development of the technico-cultural network. Thus we behold the spectacle of:

> ... this vast anatomy of an enormous *phylum*, whose branches, instead of fanning out as usual, keep on bending back more and more densely upon each other, like the monstrous growth of some huge flower that turns it on itself.[21]

Terror grips us "even to the marrow of our bones" before this threat of self-obliteration. The person feels himself menaced in his biological as well as in his spiritual structures. The "three fears" of the human race are only symptoms of our desire for "survival and superlife." It is enough here to mention these fears without entering into any detailed analysis: "fear of being lost in a world so vast that the human element seems to have lost all significance"; "fear of being reduced to static immobility within a stabilized zoological group"; "fear of being imprisoned" within a world that is "definitively closed." On the contrary, "Every particular element wishes to be clearly distinguished from every other, to be fulfilled, to be saved."[22]

Is there any remedy for this triple fear? The existentialists cry out in shocked protest against the very raising of the question. What is the use, they will say, of having come this far in order to be told that this anxiety is not ultimate, that it has a cure? For it is the core of their position to cling to the abrupt and tragic suspense of their "either-or" dilemma. It is essential to the existentialist vocation to be "inconsolable."

For Teilhard, on the contrary, there is a remedy — we do not say a solution; there is a probable way out — we do not say a certain one; for if God's creation does advance necessarily as a whole toward the final goal willed by Him, the particular acts in which the drama of our own lives is played out depend nonetheless on our own freedom.

Evolution has thrown up in its course syntheses that are more and more improbable, centers that are more and more spiritual, tending all the while along an irreversible vector. The universe is advancing upwards, and whatever ascends higher comes together, in other words, tends more and more to a center. This converging system has so far worked out to the advantage of man, who is undeniably the present vector of evolution. The emergence of reflection represents a phenomenon of centralization which makes it possible for "the thinking reed" to rise above what would otherwise crush it. Each day we rise a little farther above the infinitely great by thought and action. The emergence of a "noo-sphere" of "co-reflection" is the beginning of a new phase of evolution. The ascent continues; the world has not come to a halt in immobility.

Finally, by projecting further the same trajectory we arrive at the necessity of a "hyper-center," a higher focus of co-reflection. Through it we can find an outlet toward the irreversible. Reflection, co-reflection, ultra-reflection — such are the three lines or axes of development, proceeding from a triple choice, of an "anthropo-centrism in movement":

> Of those who brand as fantasy or poetry the interpretation of the facts that I am presenting I ask merely this: to show me . . . a perspective that integrates more completely and naturally, within the framework of our biology and theory of energy, the astonishing — and so misunderstood — phenomenon of man.[23]

Here again the existentialist philosophers will object, backed up this time by the post-Kantians, and we must turn aside a moment to answer them. The position of Teilhard, they will claim, is really an objectifying of the subject. It speaks of the human phenomenon in the same breath with biology and the theory of energy.

Let us reply by asking the philosophers of consciousness if their most authentic tradition has not always felt itself obliged to rely on a certain degree of objectification. Let us pass over the Plato of the *Timaeus,* the *Republic,* and the *Laws.* Even Kant himself, enthusiastically laying the ground-work for a future anthropology in his reflections on the Newtonian universe, deliberately "phenomenized" man, in a certain sense, without in the least believing that he was making it impossible to integrate this vision of man as an observable phenomenon with the reflexive process.

As for the existentialists, we challenge them to deny that there is a difference between interiority and subjectivism. The former thinks the world from the point of view of man; the latter exiles itself on the sinister and enchanted island of solitude and despair. In order to overcome anxiety one must, it is true, transcend the limits of a certain type of subjective meditation. But as soon as one focuses on thinking the world, a certain objective tonality reappears. (The evolution of Sartre might well be instructive from this point of view.) This whole parenthetical discussion, we might add, aims no further than at suggesting a longer study where some of the distinctions summarily sketched here might be developed to bring out how a legitimate study of man as a phenomenon by no means contradicts the primacy of consciousness.

We have now reached the starting point of Teilhard's dramatic optimism. It is the terminus of our two analyses, that of faith in the world and that of anxiety over the world. Before drawing the synthetic conclusions that impose themselves, we must further develop the significance of the Teilhardian option by confronting it with evil and death as a single entity of which anxiety is the herald.

Vigorous criticism has often been directed at Father Teilhard for his failure to speak of evil. If this means that he has not written a work dealing expressly with this subject, it is indeed true that he has not. But one might just as reason-ably blame him for not having written a treatise on astron-omy. If what is meant is that his global vision allows no normal place for evil, this is a genuine objection but it does not touch Teilhard. We neither desire nor are able to take up

73

here all of his considerations on evil. It will be enough to show that it is just as essential to his vision as anxiety.

Teilhard has preferred rather to struggle against evil than to describe it. He has drawn this distinction himself between an existential combat and a conceptual annihilation. When the entire perspective of a thinker presupposes implicitly at every moment the insistent pressure of the same question, can it be said that he passes it over?

True, evil has not hitherto been mentioned, at least explicitly. But on the other hand does it not seep inevitably through every pore, through every joint and sinew of the system within which I have taken my stand?[24]

It may even appear as greater than the good in the world: "How many failures have there been for one success, how much misery for one bit of happiness, how many sins for a single saint?" Teilhard will say,[25] as the poet has said: "How many sobs for a single note on the guitar!" If, in fact, his aim was to highlight the positive aspect of the world it would make no sense to shut his eyes to the negative side that is proportional to it: "It would be a complete misunderstanding to interpret the view here suggested as a sort of human idyll rather than as the cosmic drama that I have tried to present."[26]

Our author has sketched the diverse aspects of evil in the world at the end of *The Phenomenon of Man*. But this phenomenological study was not the proper place to study evil in itself, without giving rise to confusion. On the contrary, he pointed out explicitly the wounds of evil within us in *The Divine Milieu*, in the chapter on "the divinizing of passivities." The reader can consult it. What we would like to highlight here is the primary and ontological character of evil. At the very roots of created being which begins to organize itself against the flow of entropy, by successive gropings among improbabilities, there is something like a way of the cross in germ. The various mutations and emergences of new forms are achieved at heavy cost. Once the threshold of life has been crossed, sensitive living flesh offers a dwelling place to pain. The next step to reflection is also a step into suffering. At the human level this "metaphysical evil" is amplified by sorrow and sin, bloody tears, and so forth. Each higher plane is not, in fact, the automatic result of a lower plane in which it is preformed. Thus, on the human level, with the emergence of will and reflection appears also sin, the ethical act. Once this act has arisen it gives its own meaning to the undifferentiated disorder of the infra-human. The explanation of everything is either "above" or "up ahead."

Let us sum up the point. Evil is not localized or minimized in the world of Teilhard. It is everywhere. It is crucial. It is not an accident. It is inherent in the deep essential nature of being itself. Having disposed of the misunderstanding on the level of theory, may we be permitted for the moment an argument appealing to the emotions of our readers? Surely no one could be insensitive to evil who could write to his sister immobilized by a chronic disease:

> O Marguerite, my sister, while I, dedicated to the positive forces of the universe, was ranging over continents and seas, passionately absorbed in watching all the colors of the earth emerge, you, stretched out motionless, were transforming silently, in your profoundest depths, the darkest shadows of the world into light.[27]

At the first approach of what diminishes our forces, we can find God in no other way than by throwing off the track and eluding as best we can what is hunting us down. The more we push suffering away from us, at this first moment, with all our heart and all our strength, the closer we shall be joined to the heart and action of God himself.[28] The struggle with God against evil by means of human works is elevated to spiritual value by Father Teilhard. But there comes a moment when our own effort has reached the limit of its efficacy. It is at this point and at this point only that the transfiguration of an apparent defeat can begin. Death is the irreducible ultimate in all suffering. It is what cannot be imputed to human responsibility. It is by nature meta-physical in its essence, if not in its hour. It is the unavoid-able evil. That is why it is so apt for bringing out the final lesson of *The Divine Milieu*. Since death is the greatest mystery, if we can illumine it we can render transparent this whole mortal chapter in our lives:

> If with all his heart one loves Jesus hidden within the forces that bring death to the earth, the earth itself in sinking to its death will embrace him maternally with its giant arms and together with it he will awake again in the bosom of God.[29]

Since death is the incurable evil which cannot even trans-form us further in its hard school, since it is the end of the journey, the openness to the divine reaches to our very depths. And so death's sinister power to decompose and to dissolve finds itself enlisted in the most sublime activity of life itself. This is the meaning of the admirable prayer for making good use of death: communion with God in our very passing away.[30]

This is the "Barrier of Death" on which Teilhard, close to his own death, used to meditate, not only for himself but for humanity to come. This is the scandal of death which will become more and more unbearable as the power of co-reflection increases; the sorrow of death which cannot be consoled by devotion to the universal that humanism appeals to. In January, 1955, Father Teilhard had premonitions of a human world to come "twisting more and more out of balance towards a more and more disastrous future."[31] But precisely because such a position is decisively untenable, it must be that the world will eventually swing back to equilibrium on the side of the spiritual and the irreversible.

The point we have just made is that, like the existen-tialists, Teilhard goes all the way to the limits of inconsol-ability. He can say "Plus ego" to the existentialists as well as to the Marxists. In itself death is the supreme experience of the divine even in its apparently negative aspect, in its name-less terror. "Teach me to commune with you in dying."

Thus humanity, in a world on the verge of suicide, consciously prepared to destroy itself in the very moment of its accession to full self-consciousness, will pass over "the wall of death" only to recognizing the irreversibility of the spiritual. In this way and no other will death be conquered on the human level itself after having been so already on the "Christic" level.

Thus the perspective of Teilhard de Chardin transcends the two great currents of thought that divide up the world at present. The humanists refuse to sound the abyss; the existentialists, hypnotized by its black depths, are unwilling to look away from it even for a moment. Marxist humanism is trying its best to stifle the cry of the human person in the illusory joy of a collective-hymn. Existentialism is unwilling to cling to anything else than the pathetic clamor of abandoned individuals. Both attitudes are rigid and self-immobilized. Both are partial and even superficial analyses. Both stand for a humanity cut off from its final goal, refusing to recognize the face that is ever more and more clearly reflected in the universe.

What Teilhard proposes, on the other hand, is that we strike out again on the road, that we move ahead, in the deepest and fullest sense of the term. Beyond Kant, he joins hands again with Parmenides of Elea in his ecstasy of wonder before being, at the dawn of Western thought. His final word is that man is not radically estranged from the Absolute, but that "the human epic resembles nothing so much as a Way of the Cross."[32]

NOTES

1. Teilhard de Chardin, *Le phénomène humain* (Paris: Ed. du Seuil, 1955), p. 272; Eng. trans., *The Phenomenon of Man*, by Bernard Wall (New York: Harper & Row, 1959), p. 245.
2. Teilhard de Chardin, *Recherche, travail, et adoration* (unpublished mimeographed edition, March, 1955), p. 2.
3. See the splendid Preface of R. P. Wildiers to Teilhard de Chardin, *L'avenir de l'homme* (Paris: Ed. du Seuil, 1959).

4. Teilhard de Chardin, *L'esprit de la terre* (unpublished mimeograph), p. 25.
5. For this and the two following quotations analogous texts can be found in the published work *L'avenir de l'homme* (Paris: Ed. du Seuil, 1959), pp. 251 ff., 317 ff.
6. Ibid.
7. Ibid.
8. Teilhard de Chardin, *Le milieu divin* (Paris: Ed. du Seuil, 1957), p. 40; Eng. trans., *The Divine Milieu*, by B. Wall (New York: Harper & Row, 1960), p. 23.
9. Teilhard, *Phénomène humain*, p. 290; Eng. trans., p. 261.
10. Teilhard, *Milieu divin*, pp. 60-61; Eng. trans., pp. 38-39.
11. The author's own word, used throughout this whole section, is *angoisse*. Since its force falls somewhere between the English "anxiety" and "anguish," being stronger than the first and weaker than the second, it is difficult to capture its exact connotation in one English word. We have chosen "anxiety" as the least defective rendering throughout.
12. Teilhard, *Milieu divin*, pp. 75-77; Eng. trans., pp. 48-49.
13. Ibid., p. 172; Eng. trans., p. 117.
14. Ibid., p. 77; Eng. trans., pp. 49-50.
15. Ibid., p. 172; Eng. trans., p. 117.
16. Ibid., p. 173; Eng. trans., p. 118.
17. Jankelevitch, *Hominisation* (unpub. mimeogr.), p. 18.
18. Teilhard, *Phénomène humain*, pp. 251 ff.; Eng. trans., pp. 237 ff.
19. See the pages on the option in *Le Phénomène humain*, p. 258, and in *"L'heure de choisir," L'avenir de l'homme*, p. 231.
20. Teilhard, *Phénomène humain*, p. 258; Eng. trans., p. 231.
21. Teilhard, *Le coeur de la matière* (unpub. mimeogr.), p. 18.
22. Teilhard, *Apparition de l'homme* (Paris: Ed. du Seuil, 1956), p. 296.
23. Ibid., p. 297.
24. Teilhard, *Phénomène humain*, p. 346; Eng. trans., p. 309.
25. Ibid., p. 346; Eng. trans., p. 310.
26. Ibid., p. 345; Eng. trans., p. 309.
27. Preface to *L'énergie spirituelle de la souffrance* (Paris: Ed. du seuil, 1951).
28. Teilhard, *Milieu divin*, p. 87; Eng. trans. p. 56.
29. Teilhard, *La Messe sur le monde* (unpubl MS).
30. Teilhard, *Milieu divin*, p. 94; Eng. trans., p. 63.
31. Teilhard, *La barrière de la mort* (unpub. MS).
32. Teilhard, *Phénomène humain*, p. 348; Eng. trans., p. 311.

WHITMAN, TEILHARD AND JUNG
Ray Benoit

Hart Crane called Allen Tate to account for decrying the materialism in Whitman without having read *Democratic Vistas*. Except for Crane, I do not know who else besides Kenneth Burke has seen in *Democratic Vistas* a statement of policy that Whitman made personal in *Leaves of Grass*. But Mr. Burke's argument is convincing. The first stage of Democracy for Whitman was the getting down of governing principles. We can call this the stage of thesis, of Spirit. The second stage was the materialization of those principles into creature comforts. This would be the point we are now at, the second part of the dialectic — the antithetical stage of Matter. But Whitman does not stop here — this was Crane's point; it is not a question of well-being so much as it is of more-being. Whitman chose unhesitatingly. Yet to come out from the second stage, but beginning, is the final stage where the thesis of Spirit and the antithesis of Matter combine in a synthesis of Matter combine in a synthesis of Spiritualized Matter or Materialized Spirit. The text in question is important enough to Whitman's thought to be given at length:

For the New World, indeed, after two grand stages of preparation-strata, I perceive that now a third stage, being read for, (and without which the other two were useless,) with unmistakable signs appears. The First stage was the planning and putting on record the political

From *Walt Whitman Review*, 13 (March, 1967): 21-28. Reprinted by permission of the publisher.

foundation rights of immense masses of people — indeed all people — in the organization of republican National, State, and municipal governments, all constructed with reference to each, and each to all. This is the American programme, not for classes, but for universal men.... The Second stage relates to material prosperity, wealth, produce, labor-saving machines, iron, cotton, local, State and continental railways, intercommunication and trade with all hands, steamships, mining, general employment, organization of great cities, cheap appliances for comfort, numberless technical schools, books, newspapers, a currency for money circulation, etc. The Third stage, rising out of the previous ones, to make them and all illustrious, I, now, for one, promulge, announcing a native expression-spirit, getting into form, adult, and through mentality, for these States, self-contain'd, different from others, more expansive, more rich and free, to be evidenced by original authors and poets to come, by American personalities, plenty of them, male and female, traversing the States, none excepted — and by native superber tableaux and growths of language, songs, operas, orations, lectures, architecture — and by a sublime and serious Religious Democracy sternly taking command dissolving the old, sloughing off surfaces, and from its own interior and vital principles, reconstructing, democratizing society.[1]

The policy is poetized when catalogues of things in his poetry are invested with a powerful tone of this futurism. 'The good day will come' was inscribed on Shelley's ring, and that is the feeling Whitman's poetry generates. What I wish to show is that the day will come in more than a literary way — that the geo-biology of Pierre Teilhard de Chardin and the psychology of Jung can be used to clarify this central aspect of Whitman's thought and ground it in possibility — Teilhard would say inevitability.

The following is from Teilhard de Chardin's *The Future of Man* (New York, 1964). I quote at length again to assure that the two texts, so important to their respective authors, will be joined in our minds:

The first phase was the formation of proteins up to the stage of the cell. In the second phase individual cellular complexes were formed, up to and including Man. We are now at the beginning of a third phase, the formation of an organico-social super-complex, which, as may easily be demonstrated, can only occur in the case of reflective, personalized elements. First the vitalisation of matter, associated with the grouping of molecules; then the hominisation of Life, associated with a super-grouping of cells; and finally the planetisation of Mankind, associated with a closed grouping of people: Mankind, born on this planet and spread over its entire surface, coming gradually to form around its earthly matrix a single, hyper-complex, hyper-centrated, hyper-conscious arch-molecule, coextensive with the heavenly body on which it was born. Is not this what is happening at the present time — the closing of this spherical, thinking circuit? (p. 115)

Here what Whitman had announced in his essay is given scientific backing. The evolution of life points to just that third stage Whitman envisioned in *Democratic Vistas.* "Passage to India" poetizes this process of evolution; it is a poem about Life, the whole movement and history of life from its beginnings to the present and beyond. The poem is an inference of what is to come out of what has been given. To come is "The closing of this spherical, thinking circuit" and the emergence of an ensemble Mankind out of individual Man with the final development of "the hyper-conscious arch molecule." For just such reason is importance given in the poem to the Suez canal, the Atlantic cable, and the meeting of "man's long probation fill'd, / Thou rondure of the World at last accomplish'd." And this "planetisation of Mankind" is responsible for the tone of ecstasy that each hurried verse sounds as it spills the great message. The linkage "Tying the Eastern to the Western Sea, / The road between Europe and Asia" heralds the first glimmer of what Teilhard termed the Noosphere, a layer of mind as the zenith of evolution when physical complexity and sheer plurality are such that psychic unity will be complete and earth will arrive at its Omega Point — "the gradual incorporation of the World in the Word Incarnate" (p. 35). So, in the poem, "The true son of God shall come singing his songs" and

All these separations and gaps shall be taken up and hook'd and link'd together.
The whole earth, this cold, impassive, voiceless earth, shall be completely justified. . . .

81

II

Whitman anticipated the theories of Teilhard, only now causing excitement in scientific and theologic circles, by a hundred years. His poetry promulgates such a hyper-complex, hypercentrated network: a criss-crossing of particulars that progressively in their complexity and containment in-fold and universalize. The structure of his verse is the structure that Teilhard sees Life and evolution to follow — greater and greater complexity leading to deeper and deeper integration and unity, the particulars so many acolytes in procession of the higher integration that will inevitably follow. "The sense of the earth opening and exploding upwards into God." Teilhard writes,

... and the sense of God taking root and finding nourishment downwards into Earth. A personal, transcendent God and an evolving Universe no longer forming two hostile centres of attraction, but entering into hierarchic conjunction to raise the human mass on a single tide. Such is the sublime transformation which we may with justice foresee, and which in fact is beginning to have its effect upon a growing number of minds, free-thinkers as well as believers: the idea of a spiritual evolution of the Universe. The very transformation we have been seeking! (p. 80)

The double sense of earth's opening and God's taking root is the sense that is Whitman's verse — perfervid sense: poetry. We can now see the justice of his vision. He foresaw this 'sublime transformation' in *Democratic Vistas* which outlines the process and in *Leaves of Grass* which poetizes it. "The critical point of Reflexion in the biological unit becomes the critical point of *In*flexion for the phyla." Teilhard wrote, "which in turn becomes the point of '*circum*flexion' ... for the whole sheaf of inward-folding phyla" (p. 159). Whitman reached the critical point of Inflexion in *Drum-Taps*, the depiction of masses of men united in mind for a single purpose — "Mannahatta a-march — and it's O to sing it well" (The Noosphere is not to emerge without suffering and world upheavel: wars are the syndrome of evolution in labor.) The point of circumflexion is reached in *Autumn Rivulets,* especially in "Passage to India" where physical complexity and convergence make ready the liberation of the final sphere of mind which is to dovetail with God:

> O soul, repressless, I with thee and thou with me,
> Thy circumnavigation of the world begin.
> Of man, the voyage of his mind's return.

Return to where? To regions infinite

> Whose air I breathe, whose ripples hear, lave me all over,
> Bathe me O God in thee, mounting to thee,
> I and my soul to range in range of thee.

In such a way does "Passage to India" recount the three stages of his dialectic: (1) the setting down of principles: "the earth to be spann'd, connected by network"; (2) the realization of those principles: the canal, cable, and railroads, "the procession of steamships," "the locomotives rushing and roaring." The "Laramie plains," "the plentiful larkspur and wild onions," "the Wind river and the Wahsatch mountains" of this stage correspond to Teilhard's biosphere. And (3) the synthesis of the first two stages when

> After the seas are cross'd, (as they seem already cross'd.)
> After the great captains and engineers have accomplish'd their work.
> After the noble inventors, after the scientists, the chemist, the geologist, ethnologist,
> Finally shall come the poet worthy of that name,
> The true son of God shall come singing his songs.

With a hum like a machine and modulations like a choir, the poem shuttles the history, myth, geography, and religion of the past and present together into the future. Like the right arms of the four Evangelists in medieval art, all point to a common center, the aureole towards which everything is moving: Omega Point. It is this third stage (the Noosphere

83

for Teilhard) for which the other two stages, Whitman said, where only "preparation-strata".

A worship new I sing,
You captains, voyagers, explorers, yours,
You engineers, you architects, machinists, yours,
You, not for trade or transportation only,
But in God's name, and for thy sake O soul.

Such was Whitman's vision and such is Teilhard's hypothesis which is based, he insists (like Jung in this respect), upon an interpretation of empirical data:

By interiorising itself under the influence of the Sense of Evolution, planetisation (as the theory of complexity would lead us to expect) can physically have but one effect: it can only personalise us more and more, and eventually (as can be demonstrated by following to their conclusion all the successive stages of its twofold demand for wholeness and irreversibility) "divinise" us through access to some Supreme Centre of universal convergence. (pp. 135-136)

III

Ruling everywhere in Whitman's poetry as the structural equivalent of this theme is the principle of the syzygy which Jung sees the Self in terms of: "the tension of opposites from which the divine child is born as the symbol of unity."[2] The tension had been the romantic one: that between Heaven-Spirit and Earth-Matter. Gebhard Frei, discussing the method and teaching of Jung, describes the tension and its desirable resolution:

... not to deny or to eliminate matter, but on the one hand to spiritualise matter, and on the other to materialise the spirit by symbolisation.

The only way of achieving this ideal is to perceive the Self, for

between the male Pneuma (spirit) at the top and the female Matter at bottom, is Psyche, separating and also linking them.

84

Knowing the Psyche, the opposites become reconciled because

Matter has not been eliminated or excluded, on the contrary, 'there will be a new heaven and a new earth': spiritualised matter and embodied spirit: wholeness.

I suggest that Whitman was first torn between these pairs and then perceived in the Self their reconciliation; that the perception was, in terms of Jungian psychology, a conversion; and that the conversion in turn liberated his poetic powers. His integration of the anima or feminine earth principle through recognition had yielded the complete Self — the *coniunctio* of the masculine and feminine (spirit and matter, heaven and earth). For this reason he hails his soul ('thee of tableaus twain') over and over again everywhere in his poetry. His Psyche, while it gave him the terms of the other two as well, became propaedeutic to the third stage he envisaged outwards by having looked and seen so deeply inward. Teilhard in science today seconds Whitman's vision outwards, as Jung in psychology does the universality of his perception inward. The Self, Democracy, and the Noosphere are synonymous terms meaning one thing: spiritualized matter or embodied spirit: Incarnation. Both the Noosphere and the composition of the Self merge in these lines from 'Passage to India' which point to the fulfillment of Democracy:

Lo, soul, seest thou not God's purpose from the first?
The earth to be spann'd, connected by network,
The races, neighbors, to marry and to be given in marriage,
The oceans to be cross'd, the distant brought near,
The lands to be welded together....

O vast Rondure, swimming in space,
Cover'd all over with visible power and beauty,
Alternate light and day and the teeming spiritual darkness,
Unspeakable high processions of sun and moon and countless stars above.
Below, the manifold grass and waters, animals, mountains, trees,
With inscrutable purpose, some hidden prophetic intention,
Now first it seems my thought begins to span thee.

IV

The terms of the perception became both the thematics of Whitman's work and its structure — the structure of the syzygy, a tension of opposites united by the symbol of Incarnation which Jung found the Self to represent. When the earth approaches psychic unity, we can remember from Teilhard, its incorporation in the Word Incarnate would begin:

... the 'planetization' of humanity presupposes for its proper development not only the contracting of the earth, not only the organizing and condensing of human thought, but also a *third* factor: the rising on our inward horizon of some psychic cosmic centre, some supreme pole of consciousness, towards which all the elementary consciousnesses of the World shall converge and in which they shall be able to love one another: in other words, the rising *of a God.*[4]

Jung's is the psychology, Teilhard's is the science, and Whitman's is the literary arch-voice in America of Romanticism, the movement whose motto is "Give us both." They say in German, French, and English what Nicolas Berdyaev says in Russian, what the Romantic says in any language:

... the disciples of abstract monism ... introduce such a sharp distinction between the unique, immobile, and absolutely perfect Divinity, on the one hand, and the world of man, movement, historical destiny, tragic conflicts, plurality, and contradiction, on the other; they introduce such an antithesis and make it so impossible to bridge the gap between its poles, that they establish another extreme and unresolvable form of dualism. The only way to escape it is to deny that form of monism which recognizes only the unique and immobile Absolute as truly existing. Thus every philosophy and form of religious consciousness, which admits both the monistic and the dualist state, surmounts the hopelessness of such a dualism. It bridges the gap between the two worlds, grasps the significance of plurality, and considers the tragic experience of man and the world in relation to the destiny of the Absolute itself and the interior drama implicit, predetermined, and fulfilled in its depths.[5]

Whitman would have recognized in Jung and Teilhard kindred spirits admitting "both the monistic and the dualist state." Having written "Chanting the Square Deific," Whitman would have concurred in Jung's analysis of the alchemists' search for gold, because it was the gold for which he compounded spirit and matter as heaven and earth to produce. He panned the gold that is Christ-Self. He found the *quaternio,* the *mysterium coniunctionis* characteristic of the Self in which light and shadow, logos and eros, the masculine trinitarian symbol and the fourth feminine principle — respectively, the ideal of spirituality and the materialistic earthbound passion — form a syzygial unity-in-duality that to the Romantic is ever Parousia. Keats had said that 'Beauty is truth, truth beauty,' but it means the same thing: earth and heaven united in a paradise that is both and neither.

Such unity-in-duality would serve to remove what has been a thorn in the side of criticism — the oriental ideas in Whitman's poetry. Where do they come from? Malcolm Cowley, for example, sees in the "Song of Myself" a "system of doctrine . . . more Eastern than Western," and yet "what is extraordinary about this Eastern element is that Whitman . . . seems to have known little or nothing about Indian philosophy."[6] He didn't have to: the Self is something that everyone has, though the Western mind has split it in half by assigning ascendancy to the intellect. In the East this is not the case; "as the history of Chinese philosophy shows," Jung wrote,

it has never strayed so far from central psychic facts as to lose itself in a one-sided overdevelopment and overvaluation of a single psychic function. Therefore, the Chinese have never failed to recognize the paradoxes and the polarity in what is alive. The opposites always balanced one another — a sign of high culture.[7]

Eastern literature seems almost to hoard the secret of the Whole Self it cultivates — in "The Secret of the Golden Flower," for example, or in *The Tibetan Book of the Dead.* But the treasure is there in everyone and for anyone fortunate enough to find himself, "for this is the extraordinary thing," Jung said of "The Secret of the Golden Flower," "it is a living parallel to the course of psychic development in my patients, none of whom is Chinese" (p. 308). The East that Whitman traveled to is the rare romantic India of mountain-truth and valley-beauty — the Self. For him it was Xanadu. Whitman found the Romantic's treasure in the Self, the unity of opposites, for "we are both valley and mountain," Jung wrote, "with respect to the psyche" (p. 312). Furthermore, Jung maintained, "the union of opposites on a higher level of consciousness is not a rational thing, nor is it a matter of will; it is a psychic process of development which expresses itself in symbols" (p. 318). Gebhard Frei and Jung identify the opposites for us as spirit and matter; their union, as spiritualized matter or embodied spirit. This is the course the dialectic follows which Whitman set up in *Democratic Vistas. Leaves of Grass* is our "Secret of the Golden Flower." His rare psychic find led to his poetics; the poetics grew out of the ecstasy which Mr. Cowley describes as "a rapt feeling of union or identity with God (or the Soul, or Mankind, or the Cosmos) . . ."(p. 180). Mankind and the cosmos bring us back to Teilhard, for the course he sees them following is precisely the course of the Self as Jung describes it: toward embodied spirit, wholeness.

In Jung, Whitman would have found explicated what he meant by the Self; in Teilhard, what he meant by Mankind and the Cosmos. And what he meant was the same in all three cases: the Incarnation; in literature the symbol, the syzygy, "the tension of opposites from which the divine child is born as the symbol of unity." That is the Self for Jung and the course the universe is heading for as Teilhard sees it. Indeed, the corollary that Teilhard draws from his concepts is one that Whitman would have lustily embraced; the language is almost his own:

. . . everything is animated with a flow of Presence and of Love — the spirit which, emanating from the supreme pole of personalisation, fosters and nourishes the mutual affinity of individualities in process of convergence.[8]

The psychology of Jung and the geo-biology of Teilhard de Chardin re-enforce the literature of Whitman by clarifying its thematics on the one hand and pointing to structural equivalents on the other. Teilhard can speak for the three of them, because what he discovered in geo-biology Jung found in psychological analysis and Whitman promulgated in poetry:

Thus do I see the New Jerusalem, descending from Heaven and rising from the Earth.

Whitman would have understood the consequence of this belief too:

He who speaks these words before the Tribunal of the Elders will be laughed at and dismissed as a dreamer.[9]

Jung never dismissed any dreamer. How could he? He became too aware that like Adam, as Keats put it, the dreamer might awake from his dreaming and find it true.

NOTES

1. Walt Whitman, *Prose Works 1892*, edited by Floyd Stoval (New York: Dodd, Mead & Co., 1964), II, 409-410.
2. C. G. Jung, *Psyche and Symbol*, edited by Violet S. de Laszlo (New York: Doubleday & Company, 1958), p. 30.
3. Frei's essay, 'On Analytical Psychology,' is the appendix to Victor White's book, *God and the Unconscious* (Cleveland: World, 1961). The material quoted is on pages 261-262.
4. Teilhard de Chardin, *Hymn of the Universe*, translated by Simon Bartholomew (New York: Harper & Row, 1965), pp. 89-90.
5. Nicolas Berdyaev, *The Meaning of History*, translated by George Reavey (Cleveland: Meridian, 1962), p. 51.
6. Malcolm Cowley, " 'Song of Myself' as Inspired Prophecy," *Whitman's "Song of Myself"* — *Origin, Growth, Meaning*, edited by James E. Miller, Jr. (New York: Dodd, Mead & Co., 1964), p. 180.
7. Jung, *Psyche and Symbol*, p. 306.
8. Teilhard, *The Future of Man*, p. 60.
9. Ibid., p. 23.

C. G. JUNG AND TEILHARD DE CHARDIN: A DIALOGUE
Neville Braybrooke

Teilhard: Has not the moment passed when God speaks in the desert?

Pierre Teilhard de Chardin first asked the question in 1923. He was an ordained Jesuit priest of twelve years standing, and he was making his first journey to the Far East. All day his ship had been gliding through the Gulf of Suez, between the sharp, bare peaks of the Egyptian mountains and the slashed red sandstone and granite of Sinai.

Teilhard: How I would love to have scrambled ashore and tested those rocky slopes. But not only with my geologist's hammer. I would love to have learned if I too could hear the voice of the Burning Bush. Has not perhaps the moment passed when God speaks in the desert?

Carl Gustav Jung was born in 1875, six years before Teilhard, and outlived him by another six. In his work, he takes up the same cry.

Jung: I am concerned with the inner voice that a man can hear anywhere. Not only in the desert, but in a city or on board ship. In each of us there is imprinted an image of God, or rather "God-image". That term "God-image" is one I am particularly fond of. I have borrowed it from the early Church Fathers.

Jung was a qualified doctor and psychiatrist. At the turn

From *The Month* (February, 1968): 96-104. Reprinted by permission of the publisher.

of this century he began his researches at Burghölzli Mental Hospital in Zürich.

Jung: That is so. I am a practising psychiatrist. I am eighty and I continue to see patients. As a physician I have been privileged to see deeply into the lives of many people and am well aware that a patient's religious attitude plays a crucial part in the therapy of psychic illness. But what ages it has taken the Churches to pay any attention! I like to think of myself as a doctor of the soul.

Jung never met Teilhard. But he had read with enthusiasm many of Teilhard's scientific papers on rocks and fossils and Early Man — subjects that had always fascinated him — and Teilhard in turn was well acquainted and sympathetic to many of Jung's ideas.

Teilhard: I am very interested in his theories, in particular in his belief in archetypes and the whole Jungian concept of the collective subconscious.

But like some of Teilhard's own ideas, the collective subconscious has often proved a stumbling-block. Over-zealous disciples have made his writings about it, no less than Teilhard's about the phenomenon of man, appear far more difficult than they are. In their commentaries they have muddied the spring — and often the spring, if returned to, is strikingly clear. Both priest and psychiatrist were explorers, explorers of the within *and the* without *of man, and the links between the two. Their explorations began on immense and simple lines, and for both there was one decisive question to which everything led up.*

Jung: Is man related to something infinite or not?

Teilhard: Return to the Father, resonance to the All — can everything be summed up in that?

This is a universal question and so their thought has crossed every frontier — racial, political and spiritual. Because when a question or problem has once been formulated, a long way has been travelled towards solving it. Both Teilhard and Jung formulated theirs early — though as schoolboys both felt suffocated by institutional religion.

Teilhard was indeed a very clever boy — top in every subject, except religious instruction.

Teilhard: They told us that God blessed Jesus. But how could he, if Jesus was already part of the godhead? And those goody-goody romances about the saints and the martyrs! Whatever normal child would want to spend an eternity in such boring company? *Quelle fantaisie!*

Jung too was a clever boy, in fact so clever that he was sometimes accused by his teachers of copying his essays out of books.

Jung: Divinity classes were unspeakably dull. I wanted to know what sort of person God really was, so I slipped off to my father's library to try and discover. My father was a country parson — liberal, tolerant, and understanding — but, theologically, he was antediluvian. His notion of God belonged to the later part of the Middle Ages, like most people's in Switzerland then. I am referring to the seventies of the last century. But in the library I hit upon A. E. Bierdermann, one of whose books had a chapter on the nature of God. I was sixteen at the time. Here, apparently, was a man who thought for himself, who worked out his own views. At least that was my first impression. Yet as I read on I became disappointed. Bierdermann wrote about God's satisfaction with the world on the Seventh Day, but then went on to state that God had taken good care that the glory of paradise should not last too long. For this reason he had planted Satan in it. I asked myself, had God taken satisfaction in that too? I felt certain Bierdermann did not mean this, but was simply babbling on in the mindless way that characterised religious instruction, not even aware that he was writing nonsense.

So it was that from an early age both Jung and Teilhard knew that they were on their own. The cost of that independence of mind, of that vision which you can detect even in their earliest work, was to be isolation.

Teilhard: Will anyone ever listen to me?

That sigh comes in one of Teilhard's letters written to his cousin Marguerite in 1919. It was to recur many times more in the years that followed.

Jung: I am an outsider. Loneliness does not come from having no people about you, but from being unable to communicate the things that seem important to oneself to others.

Both Jung and Teilhard were twentieth-century voices in the desert. They had to learn to possess their souls in patience. They had to believe that their explorations, and what they found on them, were their own reward. They had to accept their mission as patient prophets. No wonder that the Old Testament figure of Job held such a fascination for both.

Teilhard: Sometimes setbacks and checks, even human setbacks, will divert our activity on to objects, admittedly human objects, which are more propitious. That is what happened to Job, whose final happiness was greater than his first.

These checks are sometimes called Fate, or Providence. Teilhard and Jung refer to them as the inner voice, the voice which hermits went out into the desert or wilderness to hear.

Jung: The Book of Job serves as an example for a certain experience of God which has a special significance for us today. For these experiences come upon a man from inside as well as from outside.

That passage comes from the introduction to Jung's study of Job, which he published at the age of seventy-seven. The same study ends:

Jung: No man is ever more than his own limited ego before the One who dwells in him, whose form has no knowable boundaries, who encompasses him on all sides, fathomless as the abysms of the earth and vast as the sky.

Teilhard: We must understand today that God no more speaks exclusively in the desert. Nor can his voice only be heard in inaccessible mountains. On the contrary, "He Who Is" dwells everywhere. It is only a matter of learning to look into the profound sphere of things, *of every thing.* The secret of the world lies wherever we can discern the transparency of the universe. We could say in fact that the great mystery of Christianity lies not in the appearance of God in the universe but in his transparence in it.

So, no longer is there any need then for men to go out into the wilderness. There are deserts in the mind where the inner voice can speak, just as God's presence is to be discerned all around. Jung and Teilhard have taught us to see with new eyes, and to listen *with new ears.*

Teilhard: *Seeing.* To see things as they are and to see them really and intensely. You might say that the whole point of life lies in that. We live in a cosmos in which there is always something more to be discovered and to see — not only physically or scientifically but spiritually as well.

Jung: I have treated a great many elderly people and have noticed that when one of them ceases to look forward to the next day as if he had centuries to spend, but looks back, then he petrifies, gets stiff, and dies before his time. Of course it is quite obvious that we are all going to die. Yet the truth is that though we accept this rationally, there is also something in us that does not quite believe it.

Teilhard had noticed something similar about Job.

Teilhard: You will remember that when hail, fire and thieves had taken everything from Job — all his wealth, all his family — Satan could say to God: "Skin for skin, and all that a man hath he will give for his life. But put forth thy hand and then thou shalt see he will bless thee to thy face". In a sense the loss of things means little to us because we can always imagine getting them back. At rock bottom perhaps none of us are fatalists.

Perhaps this reading of Job corroborates Jung's view of the psyche within us, that voice within which will not quite let us accept either the fact of our own oncoming death, or the fact . . .

Jung: . . . that death is the sad finale of everything. Let me explain. Let me explain why I have repeatedly held that psychologically death is just as important as birth, and, like it, an integral part of life. The psyche within each of us is not confined by the ordinary laws of space and time. You must have noticed this when you dream. Often you can see round corners and such things, and see into the future too. These are facts that have always existed — and only blind ignorance would deny them. Moreover these facts show that the psyche cannot be confined. It means that there must be a practical continuation of life, a sort of pyschical existence beyond time and space. That is why I have never been sympathetic to the idea of boxing life into compartments. That is why I have no use for those who refer to things as having *only* a scientific meaning, *only* a religious relevance, *only* a medical bearing. I do not like "only" judgments. As I grow older I find the dividing wall between things more and more transparent. Reality embraces everything, and I know from my experience as a doctor that medicine has not made its advances through the discovery of some trick of healing. Quite the opposite. It has evolved into a science of enormous complexity — not the least of reasons being that it has made borrowings from all possible fields.

Teilhard: When I try to analyse myself, it seems to me that my own individual hopes in an after-life in no way prevent me from devoting myself to the world. I see nothing incompatible between my calling to be a priest and a scientist. The disciplines of both help me to develop. What I oppose is any kind of rigorism, of trying to squeeze people into moulds, of trying to force their consciences. I have been reading recently a book by the Trappist Abbot of Sept-Fonds. There are some good things in it — though some I disagree with. It is all very well to talk about running a youth club with only supernatural resources, but we should not forget the other aspects of education — cooking, p.t., amateur theatricals. All these aspects of education, a full education, make us fitter to know and to serve God. There should not be abrupt divisions or dividing-walls. Christianity, rightly understood, should inform the whole man. These thoughts have come to me sitting in a trench during the lull in a bombardment. I have been using my pack to write on.

After the nineteen-eighteen war, Teilhard often spoke to student groups in Paris. On one occasion in 1924, he chose as his subject André Gide the novelist. Gide's books had been receiving a battering from many of Teilhard's co-religionists, in particular his Fruits of the Earth.

Teilhard: My object, my friends, is to show that Christian spirituality may gain from Gide's eulogy on the world of the flesh. No, I am not trying to make a Catholic of him. But through Gide, and despite Gide, I have found in his novels, and in this book especially, springs of clear water from which any Christian may drink with benefit.

That was always Teilhard's approach.

Teilhard: I want to show that God today, more than ever, does invade our universe — whatever the pagans say. He penetrates it as a ray of light does a crystal. Everything is sanctified, every layer of creation from the biosphere of flora and fauna which covers the face of the universe, to what I have called the Noosphere. That is a word I have coined — at least I think I did. Maybe my very dear friend, Edouard Le Roy, first used it in one of our conversations in the mid-1920s. You can never be sure who starts ideas. Anyway, by Noosphere I mean a layer of thought which you and I by our conscious thinking spread over the universe. You might say that the earth gets a new skin. Better still, it finds a soul.

These were controversial words. They challenged the old conceptions — and many churchmen ran for cover. But to others they represented a break-through, they answered a spiritual need of the time. Here was man preparing the way for the Lord, but preparing it in an essentially twentieth-century way. Nor was his challenge limited to scientific exploration. It went also into his books about the interior life. And indeed so much were all his ideas one of a piece, that throughout all his writing resounded the same affirmation.

Teilhard: Adoration is research, research is adoration.

Sometimes when I have said this, I have been told, "That may be so for the priest or scientist, but what about the ordinary man who works in an office or in a factory? How can a fitter's life in a modern factory of workshop be adoration? Surely at the best, at the most, his spiritual life can be no more than a hasty morning offering, some prayers at night, and a keeping of the Sabbath?" Once in China a business friend of mine asked me, "How can a commercial enterprise bring with it moral progress?" I replied, "Because your undertaking is going well, a little more health is being spread in the human mass, and in consequence a little more liberty to act, to think, to love."

That use of the word 'to love' needs emphasis. Teilhard is not using it in a romantic sense. Instead he is using it in a cosmic sense, in a way that finds an immediate response to Jung's view.

Jung: "Love bears all things", "Love endures all things". In the profoundest sense we are all victims of cosmogenic love. Whether it speaks with "the tongues of angels," or with scientific exactitude it traces the life of a cell down to its uttermost source, "Love ceases not." It gives meaning to our whole life.

Teilhard: I always like to stress "wholeness." My concern is with the whole phenomenon of man, with the "wholeness" of life with (and) its direction.

Jung: What a man cannot endure is to be aimless, without direction. To find life meaningless is to suffer from an illness. Neurotics in cities are often people who know nothing about nature, who are so isolated in their apartments that they know nothing about life in the countryside. They are quite unadapted to reality. They are like children, and it is necessary to tell them the facts of life, so to speak.

Teilhard: The universe holds together. It is all of a piece — a garment without a seam.

Jung: If you follow the story of evolution, you will find that man completes creation.

Teilhard: If you look at man's place in the world, you

will find that he is irreplaceable. That is why man's life cannot be cut into sections. That is why once you can accept the fact that research is adoration, then the whole of man's life — if properly understood — becomes worship. Science far from challenging Christianity complements it, because both the path of religion and the path of science lead upwards, and everything that rises must converge. This is happening all the time, all around us. There is no such thing as Sunday Christianity. Christianity is for Sunday and for every day.

Jung: In a book of mine about the collective subconscious, I have shown the dangers of a Sunday religion. A theologian had come to see me because he had been troubled by the repetition of a certain dream. In it, he would find himself standing and looking at a low valley covered with dense wood. In the dream he knew that in the middle of the woods there was a lake, and he knew that hitherto something had always prevented him from going there. Then one night in the dream he determined to reach the lake. As he approached it, the atmosphere grew uncanny, and suddenly a light of gust of wind passed over the surface of the water, which rippled darkly. He awoke with a cry of terror. It fell to me to remind him of the Pool of Bethesda in which the sick were bathed. I had to recall for him how in the New Testament an angel descended and touched the waters and how they thereby acquired a curative power. My theologian wanted nothing of this. All very well, he remonstrated, to speak of the Holy Ghost in a sermon, but not as a phenomenon to be experienced. All very well to read of such things in the Bible, but they had nothing to do with you or me in our everyday life.

For Jung, the spontaneous images produced by our psyche of pools and deserts were a constant reminder of the religious content in our nature — examples of the Holy Ghost speaking within, while for Teilhard, the Pool at Bethesda was an example of God immersing himself in the mystery of creation, a reminder that all the time Christ is

98

uniting himself with the forces of earth. And so closely-knit were the ideas of these two men of our century, that their writings offer us a dialogue of two minds, though there is one place where it becomes monologue. That is because Jung never confided his prayers to us in print, whereas Teilhard being a priest was often in the habit of sharing his.

Teilhard: O God, creator of heaven and earth, teach us not to forget the earth, because in earth I find hope, enrichment and virility. I surrender myself to its mighty layers, with faith in the heavenly influence which has sweetened and purified its waters. The virtues of Christ have passed into it, even unto the wildest and most unknown regions, like wildernesses and deserts. Let the attractions of the earth lead me forward, let its sap be the food which nourishes me, let its resistance give me toughness, let its power strengthen me. And finally, let its whole being lead me towards the godhead for ever and ever. Amen.

So it was that for Teilhard and Jung there was no division between their lives and worship.

Teilhard: Our world is extending its dimensions all the time. Men are discovering more and more about every sphere in it. So must our conception of God in the universe be extended, so must our range of universal prayer.

Jung: Try to see and hear the voice of inner being, what I call the 'God-image' of the psyche within us. Become conscious of the contents that press upwards from the unconscious. Be ready to listen to what they have to tell. Remember the patience of Job.

Teilhard: Remember Job. Trust always in the slow work of God.

Jung: My thoughts circle round God like planets round the sun. All life desires eternity.

Teilhard: I cannot define the world otherwise than by a gradual awakening of the consciousness. Research is precisely the frontier in the spreading of this universal consciousness. Research finds out all things, because research is adoration, research is love.

Jung: Love "bears all things", love "endures all things". These words say all there is to be said.

CAMUS AND TEILHARD
Peter Rosazza

There is one world and only one opportunity to live for the atheistic humanist. He feels that if life is worth living for himself, then he should want to make it so for others.

Albert Camus (1917-1960), an atheist, felt this way and criticized Christians for their hope in a new life after death, a hope which distracted them from involvement in this world.

What is Camus' own position on involvement? Is his judgment of the Christian valid? Should the Christian who believes in an afterlife feel less responsibility for this life? Camus' writings furnish refreshing themes for answering these questions. To look at Camus' answers and then turn to Jesuit Teilhard de Chardin (1881-1955) for his view of the Christian and involvement is to invite provocative challenges.

Many people who do not believe in God have found a reason for living in Camus' writings. His recurring message is that it does take courage to live in an absurd world but life is worth living anyway.

His writings found special appeal for the heirs of the nihilist philosophy of the late 19th century — a philosophy which began in Russia as a reaction against every type of oppression, social, political or religious. The nihilists did away with structures like the church, the state, with belief in

From *The National Catholic Reporter,* 19 February 1969, pp. 10-11. Reprinted by permission of the Publisher.

101

God, the existence of the soul and non-material beings, and with nationalism.

People, crushed by pessimism and scepticism about life bred of two world wars, found in Camus something which gave them hope in this life and showed them that life was worth living and that it was not necessary to believe in another life in order to live in this world.

Camus made explicit what so many men feel and won the Nobel Prize for literature in 1957 for having "brought to light the problems which today confront the human conscience." Life, he said, is incomprehensible with its disasters and disappointments. For example: two world wars, the Wall Street crash of 1929 and its aftereffects — and worst of all — life ends in the tragedy of death which no one can adequately explain. "Men die and they are not happy," said Caligula in the Camus play by that name, published in 1938.

Life has so little meaning because of its sad end in death, but also because of the monotony of ordinary human existence. A person gets up, dresses, eats breakfast, goes to work, eats lunch, works, takes the bus or subway home, eats, watches television, goes to bed, and the next day the routine begins again, and again the day after and so on.

But then how is life worth living if it is so meaningless and if it is bound to end tragically in death? Before Camus gives that answer, he rejects several possibilities of escape.

First, man must rid himself of any and all "nostalgia" for an afterlife which, for Camus, does not exist. One must not count on something of which he cannot be sure. He can, however, be sure of this life, so he should concentrate on it and on it alone.

Next he rejects suicide. Death, he claims, has no meaning; it is the most absurd and meaningless event we know because it does away with the greatest good, which is life. If a person kills himself, he tends to give meaning to death, but this is ridiculous because he chooses to destroy life which is the greatest good.

Finally he condemns "philosophical suicide" which is the reaction of those who reason, as did Soren Kierkegaard, that the world is so bad that there must be a God to make sense of all this mess.

But what then is left for the man who rejects either type of suicide, physical or philosophical, and who wants to continue living in this world? It is to become the "absurd man" like Sisyphus or Meursault, "hero" of *The Stranger*.

What is the absurd man and how does one become an absurd man? The absurd is a sentiment or realization which is born from an intelligent man's confrontation with a mixed-up world. On one hand man wants to know the answers to life and its problems of death, monotony, disaster and instability, but he cannot find them. He wants men to be united and to realize the possibility of communicating with others. On the other hand he sees multiplicity, men fighting against one another, a great lack of communication, tragedy in nature, earthquakes, famine, volcanic eruptions and finally death.

There are three actors, as Camus calls them, in this drama: man's desire to know and understand, the irrationality of human existence as presented by life and the world, and lastly, the feeling of the absurd which is born from the clash between the first two actors.

The man who has had this experience becomes the absurd man. He knows that this life is everything, that there is only the present. He sees that it does take courage to live in this world and that life is worth living.

But what about the world with its heartaches, tragedies, monotony and death? He scorns these. He lives with the knowledge that life will not change and because he knows this he can dominate life and its difficulties, while choosing from the many possibilities which life presents.

Camus goes into mythology to give the example of the absurd man par excellence. He is Sisyphus, who has been condemned by the gods to roll a rock to the summit of a hill. Once there the rock falls to the bottom and Sisyphus must continue to roll the rock to the top of the hill for eternity, though he knows that it will infallibly tumble to the bottom again. To know why Sisyphus has been condemned by the gods to such a punishment helps one to understand why Camus has chosen him to represent the absurd man.

After Sisyphus had been condemned to Hades, Pluto allowed him to return to life to avenge himself and while there he found life so interesting that the gods had to force him to return. "His contempt for the gods, his hatred for death and his passion for life have merited this horrible punishment which demands that he use all his forces to achieve nothing. This is the price he must pay for his love for life."

So the absurd man in our times loves life so much that he does not want to escape from it, though he finds himself condemned to roll his rock in the form of the absurdities and problems of life. He works, he is not able to change things, but because he has contempt for his rock, he can surmount life's difficulties and become happy like Sisyphus. He is happy because he emphasizes life, not death, because he scorns life's problems and is not crushed by their weight.

Camus, who published both *The Stranger* and *The Myth of Sisyphus* in 1942, intended to help man find his way as an individual in this life. But with the publication of *The Plague* in 1947 there is a noticeable progression in his thought. Camus points out that the absurd man who loves life should also want to make it better for others. He loves life, hates death and thus fights sickness, death, ignorance, famine, poverty, even though he knows that he cannot eliminate these fully and that man will eventually die.

Doctor Rieux, the principal character in *The Plague,* gives himself wholeheartedly for others during the plague which strikes Oran in Algeria. He does not believe in an all-powerful God and if he did, he would stop working to save lives and leave that to him. He even claims that "maybe it is better for God that one not believe in Him and fight with all his force against death, without lifting his eyes to heaven where he remains silent."

According to Camus, not only does belief in God diminish a man's desire to remove physical suffering, it also keeps him from working completely for the elimination of injustice in the world. Man wants very much to see unity and peace prevail in the world. However in many cases, for example in the case of communism, he has tried to attain it in the wrong way by depriving man of his freedom in virtue of a greater freedom and harmony which is bound to come, once the classless society has established itself. Whereas the communists create injustice in order to remove injustice, "historic Christianity has only answered this protest against evil with the announcement of the Kingdom, then of eternal life, which calls for faith."

But the true humanist, who is involved in the world, cannot leave the present for the future or hope for the elimination of evil and injustice in another world or in another type of society. He must work now, without pretending to solve all problems, "because . . . the world remains our first and last love." There is no other.

In 1948 Camus was invited to speak to the Dominicans at the Scaulsoir, their house of studies near Paris, and reminded them of this fact in his talk entitled "The Unbeliever and Christians." He stated that both shared a horror for evil and that dialogue was necessary between them because it was his deep hope that Christians would join with unbelievers so that "millions of voices . . . would be added in the world to the cry of a handful of individuals who, without benefit of belief or law, plead today everywhere and without ceasing for children and for men."

In our day Christians are joining with humanists in the effort to make ours a better world. They are hearing the word of God more and more clearly thanks to the renewal in the church and a growth of human conscience and awareness of others. Indeed the *Declaration on Religious Freedom* of the Second Vatican Council begins: "A sense of the dignity of the human person has been impressing itself more and more deeply on the consciousness of contemporary man." But more than 40 years ago Father Pierre Teilhard de Chardin contributed much toward a theology of involvement and much of his thought on this matter can be found in his book *The Divine Milieu.* In the case of Camus the thought on involvement had to be drawn mainly from four sources, *The Myth of Sisyphus* and *The Stranger,* then from *The Rebel* and *The Plague.* In the *Myth* Camus worked out a way of living in an absurd world; *The Stranger* is the example of how a man, though crushed by the absurdity of life, can love life. His thought progresses in *The Rebel* in which he shows that life is the greatest good and if one finds this out, then he must project it towards others, involve himself for the good of others in eliminating evil in the world. *The Plague* is the example of a "rebel," Dr. Rieux, who gives of himself completely to fight the plague and eliminate evil.

In the case of Teilhard, however, an adequate expression of his thought on involvement is contained in *The Divine Milieu.* He accepted life, he had the Christian vision of life's goodness, since all that God created is good. But he did see the truth in the criticism leveled at Christians, that belief in another world and in a better life drew their attention away from involvement in the present.

The Christian who wanted to love God and love life, work and involvement with men, found himself divided between the two. This conflict could be resolved in several ways. He could suppress his love of the world and interest himself only in objects of a purely religious nature; or he could go to the other extreme and reject the evangelical counsels in order to live what seemed to him to be a true and fully human life. A third solution was to forget the problem and be neither totally for God or the things of this life, "being imperfect in his own eyes and sincere in the judgment of men while resigning himself to live a double life. I am speaking here from experience, lest one forget."

Teilhard then gives two other solutions, the first incomplete, the other complete in that it coincides with the desires of man to serve God and men, to integrate his human activity into his love for God.

The first or incomplete solution would be to work in the world, to build, to take one's place in industry, in a profession and have the *intention* of doing good, but at the same time detaching oneself from the fruits of his work, for example, the building he constructed, the crops he raised. There is truth here, since it is important to have the intention of giving God all our works. But it is only the intention and not the results of human industry which are offered to the Father through Christ. What about them?

The solution which Teilhard calls definitive is that by his every effort man cooperates with Christ to complete the development of the world for Christ. By baptism the Christian is identified with Christ in a special way and from then on his life and Christ's are so closely joined together that he works, suffers, dies and rises with him. Christ is the Alpha and Omega, the beginning and the end of all things spiritual and material. "All things were created by him and for him. He is before all things and all things subsist in him" (Colossians 1, 16-17). He initiated the evolutionary process and guides it according to a plan which will be realized at some future point. It is from this continuing evolutionary process that man was formed, under the guidance and through the creative power of God.

Of all creatures, only man can reflect on himself, on his past and future, on the fact of the Incarnation and of his total union with Christ in a special way through baptism. Once baptized and conscious of his union with Christ and of Christ's lordship over the universe, he consciously gives back to Christ through his industry that particle of the universe in which he works. Christ himself awakens in the Christian the desire to build the world where he is, to continue the ongoing work of creation which, according to Teilhard, is far from finished; even by the humblest work of our hands we help bring it to completion.

According to this solution the Christian can take joy and pride in building, in working, in creating. Whether he is conscious of it or not, the works of his hands, the accomplishments of his efforts, come to Christ who is one with him. A carpenter who is building a new home need not only be content with giving God his intention to offer what he does. He can at the same time take pride in his work, be happy at seeing the finished product and know that what he has done is integrated into himself and by that very fact into Christ with whom he makes one.

Thus the faith of the Christian, far from causing him to be indifferent to the world, its hopes and dreams, should inspire him to work actively in the world. "Christianity is really a powerful soul which gives new meaning, charm and alacrity to that which we are already doing."

Involvement in the material world and involvement in the world of men are equally inspired by the Christian's attachment to Christ. He must do all he can to eliminate suffering and evil and the more he works at it, the "more closely he adhere to the heart and to the action of God himself." Thus the Christian does not and cannot in the name of Christianity resign himself to evil and suffering as inevitable or as necessary means of paying for sin. On the contrary, he must fight with all his strength in union with the creative power of the world to eliminate them. The true disciple of Christ does not find the will of God by passive resignation but rather becomes one with it only by working as hard as he can. In this way man approaches God and is completely faithful to his duty as a human race who does what he can for the betterment of mankind.

Just as man cannot remain passive in the face of evil, neither must he be passive in the current of evolutionary development. The time will come, if it is not already here, when he no longer has to undergo evolution but can thrust its progress ahead by his knowledge and work. In all this he must have the determination of Sisyphus or of Rieux but he works with the knowledge based on faith that his work will not be in vain, that his rock will not inevitably roll back to the earth, that the plague, once checked, will not continuously keep breaking out in other places. The Christian must be as involved in the temporal as any man, but his hope that his involvement will bear fruit in some way at some time and that Christ the Lord is working along with him should be an incentive to him to apply himself constantly to the task.

The Christian believes that Christ will come at the end of time. Teilhard states that Christians must not wait idly by until he comes, but by their activity they can hasten the coming of Christ who is present in all things. "Christ will not come quickly unless we wait for him attentively."

They need not turn their attention away from this world as if it were to be destroyed at the end of time. It will not be destroyed but made new when the presence of Christ bursts forth visibly from his creation and from the works of our hands. The biblical images of the end of the world tell us that God is going to intervene in a special way in history. He will come, not to destroy his works and the works of men, but to transform them. Christ will make himself present in the works of men so that his coming at the end of time will not be from afar but from within the universe itself. "As a flash of lightning springing from one pole to the other, the presence of Christ silently built up in the world will suddenly be revealed."

For these reasons the Christian need not feel divided between serving the world and living his faith. He is as much a part of this world in dynamic progress as any of his contemporaries. He believes as they do in the dignity of man and therefore must do all he can to eliminate evil so that man can be free. But whereas atheists like Camus hold that this life is the only one and that it ends in the tragedy of death, Christians look forward to another and better life.

Children and innocent people will continue to suffer and

die, but they will live again with Christ. Far from causing a Christian to be detached from the world, the destiny of man in Christ should inspire him to work feverously so that man may live in dignity and be in a position to hear and live the gospel which is the word of life. He must point out to a world that is not yet fully redeemed that not all the efforts of man will be fruitful for mankind.

The Christian does not know how much time there is left for him to work. He does know that he can and must unite with his fellow men, believers and unbelievers, to labor with Christ, who inspires all men of good will, for the world and for men, that they may be more thoroughly human and be better prepared to accept and enter into the newness and fulness of life which Christ offers.

BONHOEFFER AND TEILHARD
Charles M. Hegarty, SJ

In one of the most contemporary novels of our time we
read the following dialogue:

... It comes to this, Tarrou said almost casually, what interests me is
learning how to become a saint.
... But you don't believe in God.
... Exactly. Can one be a saint without God? — that's the problem,
in fact the only problem, I'm up against today. ...

In *The Plague* we find Albert Camus portraying in symbolic
and universal idiom the plight of Modern Man in a religionless world. Like Samuel Beckett's Vladimir, Modern Man is
not a saint, but he has kept his appointment and is now
yielding his eschatological hope in Godot and wandering aim-
lessly in search of meaning elsewhere. Saul Bellow's Every-
man, Moses Herzog, catches this situation in a letter he
writes to God explaining his confusion and pain.

... How my mind has struggled to make coherent sense. I have not
done good at it. But I have desired to do your will, taking it and you
without symbols. ...

Modern Man now walks through the streets of the secular
city and will wait without symbols and without idols. The
character K in Franz Kafka's *The Castle* must now dismiss
his fruitless search for entrance into the transcendent castle

From *The Catholic World*, 207 (April, 1968): 31-34. Reprinted by
permission of the publisher.

and live happily and humanly in the village below; he must accept the decree of Malamud's Fixer that "there's no such thing as an unpolitical man." Modern Man can no longer wallow in Eliot's Wasteland; he must dwell in the heart of Harvey Cox's secular city and find there his fulfillment, redemption, and sanctity. This is the image of man presented by today's artists to the theologian and to the contemporary Christian. This is the vision which the secular sixties presents and which challenges the Christian in the world.

How is the Christian to face this challenge of secularity? How can he understand and communicate with the secular age, with the "world-come-of-age," as Bonhoeffer called it? Harvey Cox replies that he should learn to live and love it in its "unremitting secularity." He tells us that it is useless to cling to our religious and metaphysical versions of Christianity in the hope that one day religion and metaphysics will arise again from their ashes. Man must let go and immerse himself in the new world of the secular city.

Since secular man is concerned with becoming a saint without God, or rather, is concerned with becoming and being a man and therefore a saint, it is from the Good News of Dietrich Bonhoeffer and Teilhard de Chardin that he can draw the impetus and vision needed to become a "worldly Christian." Due to the richly radical theology of the incarnation which permeates their thought, Bonhoeffer and Teilhard present to Modern Man a Christian opportunity for secular sanctity, or at least a Christian stance to approach this sanctity. Both of these theologians of the secular city approach essentially the same mystery, that of the existential meaning of the Christian in the world. But in their writings there is both divergence and convergence of thought as they move toward this mystery.

The central question raised throughout Bonhoeffer's writings concerns the role of the genuine Christian in the world. In his early book, *The Cost of Discipleship,* the problem is raised in the context of the Sermon on the Mount and is solved in a radically different way than the thought and vision of his later writings: His *Ethics* and *Letters and Papers from Prison* present Bonhoeffer's ultimate solution to this question, although in provisional terms. In a letter from prison on July 21, 1944, we read:

. . . I remember talking to a young French pastor at A. thirteen years ago. We were discussing what our real purpose was in life. He said he would like to become a saint. I think it is quite likely he did become one. At the time I was very much impressed, though I disagreed with him, and said I should prefer to have faith, or words to that effect. For a long time I did not realize how far we were apart. I thought that I could acquire faith by trying to live a holy life, or something like it. It was in this phase that I wrote *The Cost of Discipleship.* Today I can see the dangers of this book, though I am prepared to stand by what I wrote. Later I discovered and I am still discovering up to this moment that *it is only by living completely in this world that one learns to believe.* . . .

Bonhoeffer's fundamental search for unity, his search for a satisfactory explanation of the value of the temporal things of life (which he calls the "penultimate realities" of life), his search for the means to dismiss the traditional separation between the sacred and the secular, are all concluded and embraced by his concept of Christ as the unifying element of human experience. As he says, "It is precisely due to Jesus Christ that man is allowed to be his Creator's creature." It is by the unity found in the revelational reality of Jesus Christ that man is allowed to live within the confines of *both* the worldly and the divine reality *simultaneously.* This was Bonhoeffer's solution to the central question of man's role in the world.

Teilhard de Chardin, on the other hand, always had a problem with reconciling the world with God and man. As Father Mooney remarks about Teilhard's lifelong anxiety, "It was the discontinuity he experienced between love of God and love of world, between human achievement and the kingdom of Christ, between Christian detachment and personal self-development, between the data of revelation and scientific research." Teilhard's *The Divine Milieu,* presented a theoretical solution to this problem but did not solve his own interior quest for unity. Throughout all of his life, Teilhard was fascinated by the seductive aspect of the human. As late as 1950 he remarked:

... Today I still encounter the risks to which he is exposed who finds himself compelled by inner constraint to leave the well beaten track of a certain traditional type of asceticism not fully human, in order to search out a way to heaven along which the whole dynamism of matter and flesh can pass by way of synthesis into the birth of spirit .... To synthesize the "Upward" and the "Forward." ...

He was concerned with the question of how the Christian is to be Christified by joining the upward thrust to an Absolute with the forward thrust to personal fulfillment. In 1922 Teilhard remarked that his main purpose in life was "to fuse the Christian life with the nature sap of the universe." Hence, from his early days until his last, Teilhard sought to show that man's becoming Christ (Christogenesis) is a vital part of the universal process of the cosmos becoming Christ. This cosmic vision is distinct from Bonhoeffer's vision of Christ as the center of community, history, and nature.

Another point of divergence comes when we hear Bonhoeffer and Teilhard speak about the absence of God in the affairs of man in the world. Bonhoeffer, in speaking about the world-come-of-age, remarks:

... The only way to be honest is to recognize that we have to live in the world *etsi deus non daretur*. And this is just what we do see – before God! So our coming of age forces us to a true recognition of our situation *vis a vis* God. God is teaching us that we must live as men, who can get along very well without him. ...

Preferring to use an ancient Christian symbol of the "veiled God," Teilhard says:

... Lord, we know and feel you everywhere around us; but it seems that there is a veil before our eyes. ... May your deep brilliance light up the innermost parts of the massive obscurities in which we move. ...

Bonhoeffer, therefore, sees this absence of God as the direct impetus for reflection upon a religionless Christianity centered on Jesus Christ, the Man for Others. Teilhard sees this veiling element as the direct invitation to man by God to seek out and pursue, with the eyes of faith, the divine within the human.

But within Bonhoeffer and Teilhard's divergence of perspective is the ultimate convergence found in Jesus Christ. Teilhard once made the remark that if Christ vanishes, then what on earth have we left to justify the development of our taste for being and life. Bonhoeffer seems to re-echo this insight when he writes in one of his last letters from prison:

... the truth is that if this earth was good enough for the man Jesus Christ, if a man like him really lived in it, then, and only then, has life meaning for us. If Jesus had not lived, then our life, in spite of all the other people we know and honour and love, would be without meaning. ...

Both of these men saw that Jesus Christ was and is the center and fusing point of Christian life. Thus within their divergence of perspective and vision there is a definite convergence of thought that might be aptly described by Teilhard's remark that "... in the nature of things everything that is faith must rise, and everything that rises must converge."

As we have seen, for Bonhoeffer, Jesus Christ is the center of existence. It is in Jesus Christ, the God-Man, that reality finds its affirmation and man finds his genuine manhood. Man can no longer view reality, the reality of the world and the reality of God, as separate entities. Both are taken up in Christ who reveals the secret of God and the secret of the world simultaneously. In Teilhard we find that the world is the divine milieu in which man confronts both God and the world at the same time. In and through his contact with the world the Christian in Teilhard's vision progressively becomes Christified. Both Bonhoeffer and Teilhard employ the Pauline notion that every aspect of creation stands firm and together in Christ Jesus.

Another fundamental point of convergence can be found in Bonhoeffer's and Teilhard's reaction to the dichotomizing attitudes taken by Christian thought in the past.

Both thinkers set out to vigorously expose the separation between the secular and the sacred, the temporal and the eternal, the worldly and the heavenly. Bonhoeffer dismisses the attitude that sees the divine and the human as "mutually exclusive contraries" as well as that which amounts to "an eternal justification for things as they are." He rejects both the radical solution and the compromise and demands that the genuine Christian be convinced of his right and duty to be man before God. For Bonhoeffer, to be a Christian means simply to be a man, a man conformed with Jesus Christ, the Man for Others. There is only one sphere in which the reality of God and the world are united, and that is in Jesus Christ. He once described this unity as the polyphony of life:

... What I mean is that God requires that we should love him eternally with our whole hearts, yet not so as to compromise or diminish our earthly affections, but as a kind of *cantus firmus* to which other melodies of life provide the counterpoint. ... Only a polyphony of this kind can give life a wholeness. ...

Teilhard, likewise, demands that the Christian avoid the unreality and double-life answer to the question of being a citizen in both the city of God and the city of man. The only solution to this central Christian interrogative is a deep sense of the enrichment afforded by the world as well as the sense to see the divine within the very marrow of the human. This will enable the Christian to see "a personal, transcendent God and an evolving Universe no longer forming two hostile centers of attraction, but entering into a hierarchic conjunction to raise the human mass on a single tide." This is what Teilhard means by Christogenesis.

While both men insist upon the Christian living and loving within the context of this world, they are careful to avoid simpliste overtures to "being worldly." They both dethrone a Manichaean flight from this world and supplant it with a particular set of worldly rubrics for the Christian life. Bonhoeffer's man must be a worldly Christian, but one who is not lazily committed to self-aggrandizement. He must find his real manhood in Jesus Christ and thus become a man for others. Belonging at the same time wholly to Christ and wholly to the world, Bonhoeffer's man is taken up by God, executed on the cross, and reconciled with God in and through Jesus Christ incarnate, crucified, and risen.

Teilhard also sees the cross as the central mystery within the human-divine context of the Christian's Upward and Forward thrust to achieve union with God. He sees an inseparable alliance between man's achievement and the progress in and through his contact with the world and his renunciation in Christ. For Teilhard, Christian worldliness is a "gift begun" only to be presented in union with all creation in Christ at the final Parousia. This gift begun becomes an integral part of universal Christification. Teilhard asks in one of his lyrical prayers that "there be revealed to us the possibility of believing at the same time and wholly in God and the World, the one through the other." For Teilhard, it is only in this way that the great flame of the divine will illuminate the human, as he says, "nothing here below is profane for those who know how to see."

In reply to Tarrou's original question about being a saint without God, the agnostic Dr. Rieux, says that he feels more fellowship with the defeated than with the saints and that, therefore, what interests him is being a man. Both Bonhoeffer and Teilhard would have responded in somewhat the same manner, but they would have added another crucial clause: "What interests me is being a man and a man conformed with the God-man whose name is Jesus Christ." It is in this sense that both Dietrich Bonhoeffer and Teilhard de Chardin present secular man with a Christian opportunity for secular sanctity, or at least a Christian stance to approach this sanctity. Hence they rightly merit the title "Christian Prophets of Secular Sanctity."

VOICES OF CONVERGENCE: TEILHARD, MCLUHAN AND BROWN
Daniel J. Leary

"I would like to make plain my faith in human work and human unity, my anger against the compartments and ceilings which isolate fragments of spirits destined to be joined together, our deception in seeing ourselves imprisoned in a cell whose limits exhaust us, our anguish in seeing ourselves alone, every one of us, in astronomical space." So wrote Pierre Teilhard de Chardin, S.J., in February, 1927, giving voice to the faith that was soon to be more fully expressed in his *The Phenomenon of Man* (Harper, 1961). It is a faith shared by a select circle of intellectual radicals in our own day whose members are advancing various aspects of a new vision. These seminal thinkers are what Marshall McLuhan and Norman O. Brown refer to as DEW Lines, a Distant Early Warnings system that can tell the old culture what is beginning to happen to it. They are attempting to step out of our environment and report the changes that are occurring, changes which they believe offer both an explanation and an answer for the *dis*-ease of our times, the sense of absurdity, of anxiety, of alienation. Certainly changes are occurring — in communications, both art and information; in technology, both practical and theoretical, and in man himself — nebulous though they may be — both a change of expectations and a change of heart.

From *The Catholic World*, 204 (January, 1967): 206-11. Reprinted by permission of the publisher.

On college campuses today these changes seem to be felt profoundly. The silent generation has been replaced by the revolting one — the generation of beards, bare feet and slovenly pretensions, but also the generation of rebels with a cause which are in committed revolt against "compartments and ceilings" whether they be academic, military or social. When an intense young man told me recently that he could trust no one over thirty, I knew this to be more than the standard bid for attention that he meant he could not live and die by generalizations whose only claim to truth was that they had lasted generations. But revolt is not the total answer. The more positive approach of college students is in their genuine interest in recent trends in philosophy and psychology, religion and science, from which we are beginning to evolve a new image of man, not as a spirit imprisoned in incompatible flesh, but as an organism inseparable from his social and natural environment.

It may seem willfully bizarre to juxtapose such dissimilar figures as the Jesuit paleontologist, Teilhard; the communication theorist, Marshall McLuhan; and the amateur psychologist, Norman O. Brown; but the very range of the spectrum of speculation they represent underscores the universality of the convergence revolution taking place. Though they are all over thirty, they seem to be trusted by the younger generation who recognize in them — to use Teilhard's phrase — "the arrow pointing the way to the final unification of the world in terms of life." All three are different arrows, all proceed from different backgrounds, but all seem to be pointing toward a common center of convergence. Of the three, Teilhard's evolutionary projection is the most detailed and systematic. Consequently, in my attempt to demonstrate the essential similarity of their views, I will initially outline Teilhard's theory and thereafter parallel his concept of communication with McLuhan's and his concept of love with Brown's.

One day Teilhard came upon a friend in a remote corner of the globe. He greeted him so warmly that the other expressed surprise. "Why am I so happy?" said Teilhard, "why because the earth is round!" Such acknowledgment of the earth's curved and confining surface is a refrain that runs through the thinking of the three men. For them the earth's circularity is a concrete representation of the double and interrelated concern that forms the basis of their thinking — communications and love. According to Teilhard, the appearance of "homo sapiens" did not bring the evolutionary process to an end. Mankind, while ceasing to evolve anatomically, continues to evolve socially and culturally because the rapid development of communication media has facilitated an enriching, interpenetrating and overlapping exchange of knowledge. Just as molecules and cells combine in individual bodies, so individual human beings are now combining in social institutions. However, owing to the limited area of our planet and the increase in its population, the human race cannot survive unless mankind unites in thought and love. Therefore, we may look forward to a day in which the human species will evolve into a single, new, conscious entity, one which will no longer be dependent upon a physical body. A conscious entity of such grandeur cannot be other than — to indulge for a moment in Teilhardese — the supracosmic, hyper-complex, hyper-centrated, super-personalized, uniconscious arch-molecule, Omega Point; i.e., God.

Teilhard was profoundly optimistic about the cumulative evolutionary purpose of the earth and saw it realized in part by the rapid advances in communications:

Thanks to the prodigious biological event represented by the discovery of electro-magnetic waves, each individual finds himself henceforth (actively and passively) simultaneously present, over land and sea, in every corner of the earth. . . . The idea is that of the earth . . . becoming enclosed in a single thinking envelope so as to form, functionally, no more than a single vast grain of thought on the sidereal scale.

And Marshall McLuhan begins his most recent book, *Understanding Media: The Extensions of Man* (New American

Library, 1966), with these words: "After three thousand years of exploration by means of fragmentary and mechanical technologies, the Western world is imploding. During the mechanical ages we had extended our bodies into space. Today, after more than a century of electric technology, we have extended our central nervous system itself into a global embrace, abolishing space and time." Whether they call it a "thinking envelope" or a "global embrace," both thinkers are describing an intellectual process that goes beyond space and time. For Teilhard the thinking element is in the process of an evolutionary jump as extensions of its awareness, as its superorgans of communication, force knowledge which has been caught in the earth's curving surface to feed back upon itself. For McLuhan the emergence of electrically controlled communication media, the eyes and ears of the world, is now resulting in an implosion of knowledge. Knowledge and information envelop themselves multiple times causing an experience of the information in depth. For McLuhan this is only the first stage of the electronic age. We are now moving into the computerized stage — the cyber-cultural era. Much as we have already extended our senses and nerves by various media, we will soon be extending the whole creative process of knowing through the technological simulation of consciousness.

There are those who claim that Teilhard's view is essentially pessimistic, that according to his theory all mankind would become a single insect colony. Probably the same charge can be leveled against McLuhan on grounds that he is forecasting a future of mechanical standardization and specialism. Such views apparently reflect the conservative, middle-aged outlook of those over thirty. Even McLuhan in a recent interview admitted that "I'm not very enthusiastic about any of these events. I find certain pleasure in understanding them, but I would prefer a more stable environment." But McLuhan's imagination catches fire when he envisages not an ant hill but a society in which fragmented processes are subordinated to "human dialogue and the need

121

for over-all consideration of human unity." The two thinkers are advocating not a nightmare of rehearsed responses but an extension of the "I-thou" message of thinkers such as Martin Buber. It is not enough to use people through one's intellect. We must learn to live with people in a fully expressed community. McLuhan and Teilhard see man returned to the sense of totality he felt in his tribal days, only now the village covers the total surface of the earth. McLuhan uses the terms "feedback" and "dialogue" frequently in *Mass Media* as he discusses the vital, open relation necessary between environment and individual; and this same emphasis upon spontaneity and flexibility in the evolving human being is found in Teilhard. In fact, the priest might be speaking for both of them when he asserts that in the process of development "object and subject marry and mutually transform each other in the act of knowledge; and from now on man willy-nilly finds his own image stamped on all he looks at." Man was the message and an increasingly understood nature was the medium of his self-understanding. Now we are at a stage when McLuhan can announce that "the media is the message."

In the strictest sense, I suppose McLuhan cannot be called a visionary at all, for his role is that of observer of the most elusive of all times at any time — the present. The society of immediate communication that McLuhan reports is one that college students apparently recognize. It is simultaneously one of fully realized individuals functioning at their fullest in all directions, and an interacting mass, operating by intuition and instinct. He sees the college experience as moving away from instruction (*in-struo,* pouring in) to real education (*ex-duco,* leading out). For example, the recent phenomenon of the teach-in is actually a dialogue in which the audience becomes participant, in which the message is discovered — is created — by students and teachers working together in a charged environment.

College students who are concerned with immediate and direct communications are also frequently ardent enthusiasts

of Norman O. Brown. They share his horror of the routiniza-
tion of the imagination in the contemporary academy and in
the world at large. Their interest is but another manifestation of the convergence revolution. Brown, in attempting to
grasp the full implications of Freudianism, has come to the
same conclusion as Teilhard, that we are faced with a vital
choice. He believes profoundly that we must either change —
and change in the direction of total love — or else we must
accept dissociation from our environment and a personality
permanently crippled by repressions and enervated by fragmentation.

In his most recent book, *Love's Body* (Random House,
1966), time ceases to run and space vanishes, while man,
made newly active through totally realized Eros, attains an
apocalyptic salvation in which the complex tangles of history
and personality dissolve in a society totally free of repres-
sion. Though, as the title of the book suggests, Brown's
vision is one of the body, it treats of Dionysian frenzy,
Orphic rites and the no mind of Zen Buddhism in dithy-
rambic iterations worthy of the most exalted mystics. In his
presentation Brown has little to say about communication,
but his style of all-at-oneness (a favorite McLuhanism) says it
all. He has largely abandoned logical and linear progression,
preferring to communicate by multiple example. The sen-
tences are often fragmented gasps and the paragraphs are
individual and separated groups of thrusts at the central
issue. He relies heavily on figures of speech, aphorism and
wordplay to make his points, all time-honored devices for
the instantaneous communication of complex ideas — all
aspects of a mode of communication already employed by
McLuhan, whom he quotes frequently in the work.

In the "Filthy Lucre" chapter, the central section of *Life
Against Death* (Wesleyan University Press, 1959), Brown
holds that the love of money as a possession — as distinguished from the love of money as a means to the enjoy-
ments of life — is but the most obvious manifestation of the
many forms of division, of inertia, of *dis*-ease, which plague

our repressed society. He sees the concept of money, and the so-called rationality that conceived and maintains it, as a particularly dangerous form of "misplaced concreteness" whereby paper is hoarded rather than energy realized. In "Boundaries" which seems to me the central chapter of *Love's Body,* Brown quotes with approval William Blake's aphorism that "energy is the only life, and is from the Body . . . Energy is Eternal Delight." Both books constitute a plea and a warning that man must redirect his love, his overflow of energy, toward realizing that the self is but an extension of the other.

It seems unlikely that Teilhard would embrace the polymorphous perversions Norman O. Brown advocates in *Life Against Death,* nor would he be enthralled by Brown's espousal of tortured ecstatics from Dionysus to D. H. Lawrence. And yet Teilhard, though celibate, was profoundly conscious that worldwide charity and ultimate convergence could come only through encouraging that basic affinity of being with being, that drive toward synthesis, which has characterized the whole evolutionary process up to now. Teilhard writes *L'Evolution de la Chastete* that human love is now in its highest manifestation an "attraction aimed at reciprocal sensitivizing and fulfillment, where the preoccupation with preserving the species is gradually being founded on the more profound rapture of creating, together, a World."

Indeed, there is an ecstasy in Teilhard when he writes of the physical attractions which become spiritual attractions that break down all boundaries. The following passage from *The Phenomenon of Man* has almost the rhapsodic quality of the concluding passages of Shelley's *Prometheus Unbound:*

Driven by the forces of love, the fragments of the world seek each other so that the world may come to being . . . Love in all its subtleties is nothing more, and nothing less than the direct trace marked on the heart of the element by the psychical convergence of the universe upon itself . . . Love alone is capable of uniting living beings in such a way as to complete and fulfill them, for it alone takes them and joins them by what is deepest in themselves.

124

And Brown echoes this rhapsody as he sings of the human body which is "not a thing or substance" but "an energy system." The boundaries must break down. Insanity, according to Brown, is the refusal to admit this unity, to attempt to repress it. Sanity rests in admitting that "every person . . . is many persons; a multitude made into one person; a corporate body; incorporated, a corporation."

The reaction to such a plea is often immediate revulsion toward what the reader believes would be a mindless mass of lumpy, human pudding. But Teilhard sees his individual cells as having the capacity to give a unique and free response to value. McLuhan envisages an expanded awareness for each man. And Brown's "Garden of Delights" is composed of people whose doors of perception have been opened since they need no longer fear the death instinct, the instinct of aggression and division. Brown is not calling for disintegration, but for a breakdown of the old boundaries of ego so that a breakthrough into Utopia can take place. Seen from a certain perspective, there is nothing very new about it at all. It is as old at least as *Genesis*.

Our fall from grace is the record of our movement from animal instinct to awareness aware of itself. Now, in seeking our lost Eden, we must be aware of our thinking and loving the universe into continued being. Brown ends the chapter on boundaries with a quotation from the *New Testament*: "He that findeth his own psyche shall lose it, and he that loseth his psyche for my sake shall find it." And Teilhard can ask in *The Phenomenon of Man*: "At what moment do lovers come into the most complete possession of themselves, if not when they say they are lost in each other?"

Brown, however, draws from the East as well. Among the extracts from his voluminous sources, he quotes from *The Tibetan Book of the Dead* (Oxford University Press), the same source that Timothy Leary uses as the basis of his manual, *The Psychedelic Experience* (University Books, 1965). As Leary explains it, the Tibetan book far from being an embalmers' guide "is a detailed account of how to break

125

out of personality into new realms of consciousness."

Both Brown and Leary use such sources in an attempt to free men from the games they play. That, it seems to me, is what the youngsters are trying to do. The best of them are in revolt against our games and the roles we would impose upon them. They have no limiting goals; they just want to know what is going on and where the action is.

McLuhan links the themes of communications and love when he mentions that he read a portion of *Finnegans Wake* (Viking Press, 1959) to a young man, and at the end of the reading the young man said: "When you take L.S.D. the whole world takes on a multidimensional and multisensuous character of discovery. When I listened to *Finnegans Wake* I got the same experience as L.S.D."

The young today want involvement of their total being; if they can't have a teach-in, they prefer a drop-out. "Finn again is awake" — Joyce's pun tells us that only when the ego is absorbed in a "multidimensional and multisensuous" universe can we return to the days of the great mythological Finn, can we return to a time of total ecological awareness and animating imagination. To become conscious of our participation in the creation of the phenomenal world is to pass from passive experience — perception as impressions on a passive mind — to conscious creation, and creative love.

What is the cause of our *dis*-ease, of our sense of absurdity? In one way or another, all the thinkers I have mentioned would agree with Alfred North Whitehead's diagnosis of "misplaced concreteness." He held that because we had put crippling rational restraints on our sense and imagination, nature for us had become "a dull affair, soundless, scentless, colourless; merely the hurrying of material, endlessly, meaninglessly." The remedy also seems to be clear — a return to Romanticism, if by Romanticism we mean a rejection of boundaries in nature, in society; an acceptance of mystery, of new possibilities; and the projection of youth's hope and freshness into the adult sphere. To be able to experience the world, we must avoid the "rehearsed response" that W. H. Auden saw at the heart of our age of anxiety; to achieve ourselves, we must first experience a change of expectations and a change of heart. This visionary trio is telling us: "Unless we become as little children, we shall not enter into the kingdom of heaven."